A NARCISSIST DESTROYED MY LIFE

A Narcissist Destroyed My Life

NICOLE DAKE

Other works by Nicole Dake

Trauma Survivor's Guide to Coping with Panic Attacks
Happy. Healthy. Rich. The smart mom's guide to living your best life
The Way Things Go – A book of poems
How to Self-Publish your E-book
Daily Positive Affirmations

Contents

Chapter 1

Prevalence of Narcissism

It may seem that, in recent years, narcissistic abuse is on the rise. Is that true, or is the issue of narcissistic abuse just getting more attention now than it did in the past?

Part of the reason that narcissism wasn't so prevalent in previous generations has to do with the history of the disorder, and the diagnostic criteria.

According to Very Well Mind,

In 1980, narcissistic personality disorder was officially recognized in the third edition of the Diagnostic and Statistical Manual of Mental Disorder and criteria were established for its diagnosis.

This means that, practically speaking, someone would not have been formally diagnosed as a narcissist before 1980, although there was some research prior to that time. So, although narcissism itself is not new, the diagnosis and treatment of this personality disorder is new.

If your parents grew up before the 1980's, that means they would likely not have been diagnosed formally by a mental health professional as having Narcissistic Personality Disorder, unless they sought treatment later in life.

Whole generations of people were unwittingly raised by narcissists. That is why today, many of us in our 30's, 40's and beyond are seeking treatment for issues caused in our childhoods while we were raised by these narcissists.

According to a study published in the <u>National Library of Medicine</u>,

Prevalence of lifetime NPD was 6.2%, with rates greater for men (7.7%) than women (4.8%).

Although these statistics show that narcissists represent a very small portion of the population, it is interesting to note that narcissism and narcissistic abuse seem to be growing problems in our society.

Why is everyone's ex suddenly a narcissist?

If you are on social media at all, you may notice that lately everyone and their brother seems to be calling their ex a narcissist after a break-up. If you have been through a relationship with a true narcissist, most likely you will want to empathize with them.

However, you may also be wondering if your friend Susie on Instagram's ex really is a narcissist, or if Susie is just exaggerating what happened to her.

According to <u>Psychology Today</u>,

People who have experienced the trauma that comes from actual psychological abuse have been empowered by a greater understanding of terms like narcissism and narcissistic abuse. These terms often cast light on an experience that felt too confusing and painful to explain in the moment. But true narcissistic abuse is so much more than just arrogance. Those who have experienced psychological and pathological abuse at the hands of someone who lacks empathy and conscience would never again mistake the spiritual warfare they endured with the behavior of someone who simply acted like a jerk. The overuse of this word to describe every ex who broke someone's heart is dismissive of the experiences of those who know the pain of narcissistic abuse.

When we look at the prevalence of narcissistic abuse in society, we must ask ourselves, are these acts being committed by a small number of people simply moving from one victim to the next, or is the percentage of narcissists in society actually increasing?

According to <u>Forbes</u>, *"Recent studies have shown that 6% of the population have experienced clinical NPD (narcissistic personality disorder) at some point in their lives. But many more experience non-clinical symptoms."*

The statement that other people have non-clinical symptoms means that although some people may not meet the full criteria for Narcissistic Personality Disorder according to Psychology, they still have some narcissistic traits. This could also explain the reason that there are seemingly so many more narcissists now than ever before.

<u>Raging Female</u> asks the question,

So how did it get so bad, and why has there been an explosion of narcissistically abused, middle-aged adults still trying to recover from their childhood? It's become more common to have a narcissistic parent, and it's not unusual if both your parents are narcissistic since narcissists tend to flock together—birds of a feather and all that.

We're also noticing that childhood emotional neglect from having emotionally unavailable parents has had a shocking increase. Maybe because we're more aware of it now, or maybe because we're more focused on personal development and emotional growth. I can tell you it's not because women started working outside the home. For kids like me, we had no desire to be trapped at home alone with our mother any more than we had to be.

What is clear from people presenting in therapy is that there are more people seeking help for narcissistic abuse than ever before. Since this is a growing issue, it is important for us to learn to cope with narcissists, and the chaos that they sow in their wake.

Raging Female continues,

The pendulum swung way high for the Baby Boomers. They got the best of everything after the war, and because of that, they have an even higher percentage of narcissists who took it all for themselves and left nothing for their children or grandchildren. Then they scream and complain about how our generations don't know the meaning of hard work and that we're weak with all our feelings they don't understand.

It could be that, growing up in unique conditions after World War II, the Baby Boomers had a unique childhood experience that led them to being more narcissistic overall than any generation before or since.

Raging Female continues,

Narcissistic abuse has been going on for centuries, and it's as ancient as it gets. However, the Baby Boomers are the most narcissistic parents in history (in my opinion). I've always suspected this, and today I watched <u>this video with my favorite leading expert Dr. Ramani</u> on narcissistic abuse, and it happens to be her opinion too.

We have all seen the problems that Boomers have caused in society, but they have caused trouble on the home-front too. More often divorced than previous generations, the "Me" generation perhaps also focused less on the happiness of their children. Broken families have ways of leaving children behind and focusing less on their inner emotions growing up.

Photo by Unsplash

Signs of Narcissism

People that we commonly refer to as Narcissists have what, in psychology, is called Narcissistic Personality Disorder.

In college, I took a class about personality disorders, and we learned that Narcissists are the least likely to seek therapy for personality disorders. This stems from the fact that their narcissism isn't really negative for *them*, just for the people around them. Narcissists never feel like they have a problem, much less that they are creating problems for others.

Narcissists are self-absorbed and think that the world revolves around them. To them, other people are treated as one-dimensional objects. In their minds, other people are just characters in the narcissist's story.

According to the Mayo Clinic,

Signs and symptoms of narcissistic personality disorder and the severity of symptoms vary. People with the disorder can:

- *Have an exaggerated sense of self-importance.*
- *Have a sense of entitlement and require constant, excessive admiration.*
- *Expect to be recognized as superior even without achievements that warrant it.*
- *Exaggerate achievements and talents.*
- *Be preoccupied with fantasies about success, power, brilliance, beauty or the perfect mate.*
- *Believe they are superior and can only associate with equally special people.*
- *Monopolize conversations and belittle or look down on people they perceive as inferior.*

- *Expect special favors and unquestioning compliance with their expectations*
- *Take advantage of others to get what they want.*
- *Have an inability or unwillingness to recognize the needs and feelings of others.*
- *Be envious of others and believe others envy them.*
- *Behave in an arrogant or haughty manner, coming across as conceited, boastful and pretentious.*
- *Insist on having the best of everything — for instance, the best car or office*

At the same time, people with narcissistic personality disorder have trouble handling anything they perceive as criticism, and they can:

- *Become impatient or angry when they don't receive special treatment.*
- *Have significant interpersonal problems and easily feel slighted.*
- *React with rage or contempt and try to belittle the other person to make themselves appear superior.*
- *Have difficulty regulating emotions and behavior.*
- *Experience major problems dealing with stress and adapting to change.*
- *Feel depressed and moody because they fall short of perfection.*
- *Have secret feelings of insecurity, shame, vulnerability and humiliation.*

Learning to recognize these signs as red flags in toxic family members, or relationship partners will give you a clue that someone in your life may be a narcissist. However, it is important to **remember that for a formal diagnosis of Nar-**

cissistic Personality Disorder, the person themself would have to present for therapy.

Do these traits remind you of someone in your life?

If so, you may be coping with a narcissist.

Recognizing narcissists for what they are is the first step towards learning how to manage relationships with these difficult people and finding help for your mental health as a result of these toxic relationships.

Narcissistic Parents

Chapter 2

Narcissistic Parents

Many of us grew up with narcissistic parents and have had to deal with a lifetime of narcissistic abuse, for which we are seeking healing today. Relationships with narcissistic parents are difficult and cause a host of issues for children growing up in a family with a narcissist.

Each child in the family may have a somewhat different experience with the narcissistic parent, and some will never seek treatment because they are so enmeshed with the narcissistic parent.

According to Psychology Today,

A narcissistic parent can be defined as someone who lives through, is possessive of, and/or engages in marginalizing competition with the offspring. Typically, the narcissistic parent perceives the independence of a child (including adult children) as a threat, and coerces the offspring to exist in the parent's shadow, with unreasonable expectations. In a narcissistic parenting relationship, the child is rarely loved just for being herself or himself.

Children of narcissistic parents may grow up with unrealistic expectations being placed on them, cope with manipulation, and deal with a host of other relationship issues with their parents.

According to Psychology Today, there are 10 signs of Narcissistic Parents:

- *Uses/Lives through one's child*
- *Marginalization*
- *Grandiosity and Superiority*
- *Superficial Image*
- *Manipulation*
- *Inflexible and Touchy*
- *Lack of Empathy*
- *Dependency/Codependency*
- *Jealousy and Possessiveness*
- *Neglect*

If you notice several of these signs in your relationship with your parents, then that is a good indication that they may be a narcissist.

Even if your parents just have some narcissistic traits without being a full-blown narcissist, the odds are pretty good that you are coping with fallout from a difficult childhood. You are probably asking yourself what you did wrong to deserve their mistreatment, or why your parents don't love you in a healthy way.

According to Dr. Jonice Webb (Running On Empty, page 16):

Narcissistic parents don't really recognize their children as separate from them. Instead, they see their children as little extensions of themselves. The needs of the child are defined by the needs of the parent, and the child who tries to express his needs is often accused of being selfish or inconsiderate.

Children of narcissists are valued the same way that the narcissist's possessions are valued. The narcissist wants to have perfect children who are a good reflection on them. These children are often treated as accessories, to be paraded around in public, and ignored or neglected in private.

Narcissists may not actually want children, and only have them out of a social expectation to do so. They want the image of being the perfect parents with the perfect family, but since they are so self-absorbed, the task of doing the actual parenting becomes tiresome for them.

photo by Unsplash

How I figured out that I came from a family of narcissists.

It was 2016, and I was pregnant with my daughter, River. My mom was planning a baby shower for me, which I had told her I didn't want or need, but I had finally relented after her repeated urging and insistence. She had decided to invite a bunch of people that I had no desire to see, including an aunt of mine who had recently been calling me and leaving threatening voice messages, so I wrote an anonymous Reddit post about it to vent my frustrations.

After writing about the situation so that I could vent, I was referred to another subreddit in a comment, called "Raised by Narcissists." Before I wrote anything on Raised by Narcissists, I read through a bunch of the postings there, all the time thinking, **this is me**.

Before that, I had never realized how much of a problem my family relationships were. Sure, being in my 30's, I knew that they were bad. My mom had this tendency of always making my problems worse through shame, blame, and endless "what if's."

My extended family treated me like I was still a troubled teen, long after I had ceased being either one of those things. They always brought up the worst things I had ever done at family gatherings to rub them in my face.

I avoided all family gatherings as much as possible, but I couldn't avoid my own baby shower. So that is where the problem came in. I made sure to have my best friend co-host with my mom so it didn't get too out of hand. I invited all my friends. It ended up being fine, but everything that I had read from Raised by Narcissists was still in the back of my head.

A few months later, I found out some things that my mom and sister had done years ago that put my teen daughter into danger as a young child. After my daughter mentioned it, I stewed over the fact that my mom and sister had lied to me for years.

They endangered my child repeatedly, and they lied to me about it.

For months, I tried to let it go, but I just couldn't.

Throughout the next year, I tried to set boundaries with my family to no avail. I talked to them less and less, noticing the toxic traits more every time. Finally, I just stopped talking to them altogether because I couldn't take it anymore.

Hurt me, that's one thing. But hurt my child, that's quite another. I had a new baby and I needed to keep her safe from toxic people.

Conclusion

Coping with a Narcissistic family is difficult and often painful. If someone in your life is exhibiting the signs of being a narcissist, it is important to seek support either in support groups, from your partner or friends, or from a therapist.

In the latter half of this book I will discuss coping strategies for dealing with the narcissist in your life, setting boundaries with them, the decision to cut off contact, as well as some tools for healing that can be used in your own life.

Chapter 3

Why am I so Traumatized by Narcissistic Abuse?

Long-term interactions with a narcissist can make you doubt yourself

When you are coming out of a relationship with a narcissist, it can feel like you are shattered into a million pieces. This is a perfectly normal way to feel, under the circumstances.

Although they may seem charming at first, narcissists are actually very dangerous people, and being in any kind of relationship with them can be damaging to your self-esteem. This includes romantic relationships, family relationships, work relationships and friendships.

Effects of Narcissistic Abuse

Depending on how the relationship played out, and how long you were in the relationship with the narcissist, there can be lasting effects on your mental health.

According to Very Well Mind, these can include:

Anxiety

Depression
Post-Traumatic Stress
Loss of Sense of Self and Self-Worth
Inability to Forgive Yourself
Difficulty Sleeping
Headaches
Stomachaches
Nightmares
Memory Loss
Emotional Lability
Trust Issues
People Pleasing
Self-Destructive Habits

Several of the consequences of living with narcissistic abuse listed here—Anxiety, Depression and PTSD—are psychological disorders themselves.

The consequences of these disorders that may develop while living with a narcissist take place because there are changes that have taken place in your brain in attempting to cope with the abuse that you endured.

What can narcissistic abuse do to your brain?

When you suffer from narcissistic abuse, especially for a pro-longed amount of time, or when you are intensely involved with the narcissist on a day to day basis, coping with their crazy-making behavior can make changes to the way that your brain responds to stressful situations.

If you are living with a narcissist, you are often coping with situations so far outside the norm that trying to wrap your mind around them in a normal way can prove to be impossible. Because of this, your brain will form new neural connections to react in a way that is compatible with the type of stressful situations that you are experiencing.

According to Psych Central, Long-Term Narcissistic Abuse Can Cause Brain Damage:

According to Goleman (2006), everything we learn, everything we read, everything we do, everything we understand, and everything we experience counts on the hippocampus to function correctly. The continual retention of memories demands a large amount of neuronal activity. In fact, the brains production of new neurons and laying down connections to others takes place in the hippocampus (Goleman, 2006, p. 273). Goleman also stated, The hippocampus is especially vulnerable to ongoing emotional distress, because of the damaging effects of cortisol (p. 273). When the body endures ongoing stress, cortisol affects the rate at which neurons are either added or subtracted from the hippocampus. This can have grave results on learning. When the neurons are attacked by cortisol, the hippocampus loses neurons and is reduced in size. In fact,duration of stress is almost as destructive as extreme stress. Goleman explained, Cortisol stimulates the amygdala while it impairs the hippocampus, forcing our attention onto the emotions we feel, while restricting our ability to take in new information.

Yes, you are reading this right. Living with a narcissist for any amount of time can take such a toll that it is actually changing the way that your brain functions. This can explain a lot about how you feel that you have changed as a result of such a toxic situation.

Of course you feel like you have changed, because your brain itself has changed because of this damaging relationship.

If you think you aren't reacting in a way that fits with your personality, the changes to your brain can go a long way in explaining the changes in your personality as well. As you are conditioned over time to play along with the narcissist, it changes your neural pathways and the way you react to situations as a result.

Living with a narcissist on a day to day basis can take a huge emotional toll on survivors. This can play out in a variety of ways over time.

It is important to remember to be gentle with yourself as you are searching for healing! Beating yourself up or blaming yourself is not going to help. Always remember, it isn't your fault that the narcissist abused you. Narcissists abuse anyone who is closely in their circle, that is just what they do.

The problems in the relationship aren't about something being wrong with you, although the narcissist tried to convince you to the contrary! The problem is with *them*, and them only.

Since Narcissists have Narcissistic Personality Disorder, their disordered behavior has unfairly disrupted your life.

The sooner that you can stop blaming and shaming yourself for being in this relationship, the better!

Chapter 4

Narcissistic Traits Explained

There are some key narcissistic traits that can be a part of relationships with a narcissist. When you notice these signs in a relationship with a family member or a partner, they should be huge red flags.

Many of the harmful behaviors that you will see narcissists exhibit stem from what is called a 'lack of empathy.' Having a lack of empathy means that they don't identify with the feelings of others in the same way that normal people do. The narcissist is psychologically predisposed not to care about the feelings of others. They may pretend to care about your feelings for a time, but after a while their facade of pretend caring is going to crack and you will see their true nature.

According to <u>Very Well Mind</u>,

A lack of empathy isn't always easy to detect, but there are a few signs that can help you determine if you or a loved one might not be empathetic:

- *Being extremely critical of other people*
- *<u>Blaming the victim</u>*
- *Not <u>forgiving people</u> for making mistakes*
- *Feeling like other people are too sensitive*

25

- *Not listening to other people's perspectives or opinions*
- *An inability to cope with emotional situations*
- *Lack of patience for other people's emotional reactions*
- *Reacting with impatience or anger when frustrated with other people*
- *Feeling baffled by other people's feelings*
- *Believing that negative things won't happen to you*
- *Not thinking about or understanding how your behavior affects other people*

Empathy isn't an all-or-nothing quality. Think of it as a continuum. Some people are naturally more empathetic, while others are less so. Other factors, including situational variables, can affect how much empathy people feel at any given time.

Some of the destructive qualities that you may commonly see a narcissist display as a result of their lack of empathy for others are manipulation, gaslighting, and perfectionism.

What is Manipulation?

Manipulation is one of the key tactics that a narcissist will use to shape their relationships to their control. When a narcissist manipulates you, they are trying to get you to think or behave in a certain manner that is consistent with their expectations of you.

According to WebMD,

Manipulation is the exercise of harmful influence over others. People who manipulate others attack their mental and emotional sides to get what they want. The person manipulating — called the manipulator — seeks to create an imbalance of power, and take advantage of a victim to get power, control, benefits, and/or privileges at the expense of the victim.

When you are being manipulated, the narcissist is trying to get their way at all costs. They may ask you for favors, ask you to change your opinion on things that are important to you, or to compromise your values. They will make you believe that continuing the relationship is contingent upon you making these changes to placate them.

WebMD continues,

Manipulators have common tricks they'll use to make you feel irrational and more likely to give in to their requests. A few common examples include:

- *Guilt*
- *Complaining*
- *Comparing*
- *Lying*
- *Denying*
- *Feigning ignorance or innocence*
- *Blame*
- *Mind games*

A narcissist will use some or all of these manipulative tactics to get you to do what they want.

In some instances, they will also try to rewrite past history to fit their narrative. If you disagree with them, they may feign ignorance or blame you for what happened, even when it is clearly not the case.

Narcissists are good at using guilt, blame and shame to make you feel like you were wrong and they were right. This can happen with arguments that have taken place, or in instances where your behavior didn't fit with what they wanted you to do.

Often, the narcissist will speak up about the things that they find are 'wrong' with you at length in front of other people, attempting to get you to change and to shame you into agreeing with them. This is the narcissist's way of enlisting others to believe in their side of the story, while totally disregarding yours.

Narcissists are very good at getting other people to believe their side of the story by speaking up and acting hurt by something that you did. They play the victim to get others on their side, and to aid unwittingly in their crazy-making.

When narcissists are in groups, they may be more cruel than usual, as being around their friends and cronies emboldens them.

Often, when you are reading about narcissistic abuse, these other people that the narcissists enlists in helping them shame you into compliance are called 'flying monkeys.' These are people that have previously been groomed by the narcissist to agree with whatever they say. The flying monkeys are being manipulated by the narcissist as well.

According to <u>Narcissistic Abuse Support</u>,

The term 'flying monkeys' is another way of saying 'abuse by proxy' or having someone else do the bidding of in this case a narcissist. The term flying monkey was coined after the flying monkeys in the Wizard of Oz that were under the spell of the Wicked Witch of the East, to do her bidding against Dorothy and her friends.

This common narcissistic tactic uses friends and family of the victim to spy on them, spread gossip while painting the narcissist as the victim and their target as the perpetrator. Flying monkeys can be your friends, family, coworkers or the narcissist's friends, family, or coworkers before you got there. To maintain the illusion of the power they have over you, the narcissist will employ the use of third parties, through which they will attempt to continue control and manipulate you.

Sometimes, when you have grown up as the child of narcissistic parents, and then get into a relationship with a narcissist as an adult, the two narcissists will play off of each other to control you. Then, they will tell other people in your sphere about how crazy you are, and how much is wrong with you, so that they are in effect alienating anyone in your life that you could potentially turn to for help when the relationship begins to sour.

My ex and my <u>sister</u> were both always very sarcastic, and they would play off each other in social settings to make jokes at my expense. Everyone else just thought it was funny and didn't realize that they were being used to listening to these jokes at my expense.

It was hurtful and invalidating, and no one ever spoke up against them on my behalf. They had all been turned into flying monkeys by my narcissistic ex and my narcissistic family.

<u>Narcissistic Abuse Support Continues,</u>

Narcissists begin grooming your friends and family from the moment they meet them. In the beginning, the narcissist is testing them and your relationship with them to see how strong the bond is.

At first, they may tell your friends and family 'how much they love you and how they think you are soul mates'. This test will be to see if your friends go running back to you with this information.

This is sweet and loving on the surface but behind the scenes, the mind of the narcissist is testing your friends to see if they are controllable.

Over time the messages they are feeding your friends and family may start to contain a little nugget of truth, only now the narcissist is poking fun at you behind your back. They may highlight something like "Tracy is such a good storyteller, I never know when she is making something up."

What this test does is plant the seed for later when you start to tell your friends stories about the narcissists lies, cheating and behaviors. The seed of doubt has now been planted and your own friends and family will not believe the things you say about the narcissist when they go from good to bad. Mission accomplished.

The purpose of turning your family and friends into the narcissist's flying monkeys is to isolate you. The narcissist wants everyone in your life to be on their side instead of yours if any type of conflict starts to arise between you, or their relationship with you starts to fall apart.

By subtly controlling the dialogue with everyone in your life, the narcissist is removing your support system. This leaves you all alone, questioning your sanity, and with no one else to turn to with your concerns about the relationship with the narcissist.

What is Gaslighting?

Photo by Wix

Gaslighting has become a common term lately, and this can happen in any type of relationship; romantic relationships, parent-child relationships, work relationships, you name it.

As someone who <u>grew up with a narcissist</u>, I never realized how bad my mother gaslighted me until I was an adult.

Sometimes, the more time and space we get away from our parents, the more we realize their unhealthy behavior patterns. Growing up, our families may have been dysfunctional in ways that we thought were normal at the time. It is only later we realize just how unhealthy it was living with a narcissist.

Gaslighting is a behavior that is common to narcissists, although it can be an unhealthy communication style used by anyone.

According to <u>Psycom</u>,

If you're not sure what it is, simply put, gaslighting is a form of psychological manipulation in which someone makes another person doubt his or her perceptions, experiences, memories, or understanding of events. Gaslighting can really mess with a person's mind and it is especially harmful when it comes from your own family — your parents in particular.

My mother, and the extended family on her side, gaslighted me for years. Anytime someone did something hurtful, yelled at me, talked down to me, or made horrible comments, she would just tell me it was my fault for being *bad*. She never stuck up for me when I was in a bad situation for any reason. She would blame and shame me instead. This is very common narcissistic behavior that you may have experienced in a relationship with a narcissist as well.

According to <u>Psycom</u>,

In the family environment, there are three primary types of gaslighting, according to Malkin:

Narrative gaslighting, in which a child might remember things a certain way and the parent changes the story and tries to convince the child it happened their way.

Emotional gaslighting, in which a parent reacts to a child as though his or her feelings are wrong or don't make sense when they actually do — which is problematic because "our feelings are very close to our sense of self," Malkin notes.

Personal gaslighting, whereby a parent undermines a child's sense of his or her own capacity or trust in him- or herself. "This is often the most insidious form because it manipulates you to think that what you know about yourself is not true," Malkin says. "It also undermines your self-esteem and trust in yourself."

Keep in mind: "Gaslighters are not born — they learn it somewhere," Stern says. So, a parent who gaslights his or her children may have experienced it or witnessed it in their own life.

My mother used all of these forms of gaslighting with me over the years, but mostly emotional gaslighting. Any time I felt sad about something, she would just tell me not to be sad. If something bad happened to me, she would tell me it was my fault.

Scraped knee? My fault. Bad grades? My fault. My dad hit me? My fault. Starving orphans in Africa? My fault. You get the picture.

My mother would never take my side in anything. She never stood up for me. She just liked to tell me that things were my fault. It absolved her of any responsibility for helping me to better my situation. This is something that narcissists will do frequently.

Another gaslighting tactic is to make you feel like you are crazy. The person gaslighting you will tell you that your reaction to some situation is wrong. They tell you that you are crazy for reacting the way you have. This will happen over and over across a wide range of situations, usually when you exhibit an emotional reaction to something that happens.

Let me break it down for you. Pretend that mom yells at you for not taking out the trash. Your brother was supposed to take out the trash. You start to cry for being yelled at. Mom will probably tell you to stop crying, and that it was never your brother's chore, it was yours all along. The narcissist has effectively rewritten the story of what happened and made everything your fault. This is a classic example of gaslighting.

According to <u>Medical News Today</u>, here are some other examples of gaslighting:

Countering: *This tactic involves an abusive person questioning someone's memory of events, even though they have remembered them correctly.*

Withholding: *This describes someone who pretends not to understand something, or who refuses to listen.*

Forgetting: *This involves an abusive person pretending they have forgotten something, or denying that something happened.*

Trivializing: *This refers to an abusive person making someone's concerns or feelings seem unimportant or irrational.*

Diverting: *This technique occurs when an abusive person changes the subject, or focuses on the credibility of what someone is saying rather than the content. Some people also call it "blocking."*

Years later, if you bring up something traumatizing from childhood, your narcissistic parents will likely either tell you they don't remember, or that it never happened. This is another way that they will use gaslighting to rewrite history, even years later.

Narcissists never want to take responsibility for their actions. Everything that happens is always your fault. Situations always manage to become just about your reaction, instead of what actually happened.

Effects of Gaslighting

Since gaslighting, especially long-term, can make you feel crazy, this can lead to a great deal of trauma for the person being gaslighted. The trauma can be heightened if the gaslighting happened in childhood as well before you have formed a healthy sense of self.

According to Medical News Today,

Gaslighting is a form of abuse that involves a person deliberately causing someone to doubt their sanity. This may cause feelings of confusion or powerlessness. The long-term effects of gaslighting include trauma, anxiety, and depression.

Yes, you read that right.

Gaslighting is a form of **abuse**.

When you have parents that are abusive, it is obvious that this type of behavior on their part can easily lead to trauma, or manifest as PTSD in adulthood, as well as anxiety and depression while you are in the situation.

Sometimes, the person gaslighting you will purposely say something to cause a reaction in you in front of other people. They do this to provoke a response, and to get other people to think you are crazy. Other people will think your response is vastly out of proportion to the situation, not realizing that you may have suffered years of abuse at the hands of the narcissist.

This will make you further doubt yourself.

Conclusion

Gaslighting is an abusive behavior that causes you to question yourself, your feelings, and your memories of events that have taken place in the past.

When a narcissist has been gaslighting you, it can lead to anxiety, depression and PTSD, for which it is helpful to seek therapy. You may also want to think about setting firm boundaries, limiting contact, or going no contact.

How Perfectionist Parents Kill Their Children's Dreams

My dad was a perfectionist, and I spent my whole childhood feeling like I would never measure up to his expectations of me.

Photo by Mesh on Unsplash

When I was a kid, my dad was super into chess. He taught my sister and me how to play chess when we were in Elementary school and started a chess club at our school.

For some reason that I will never understand, he also put me into chess lessons with the State Chess Champion. Once a week, I would go and study all the moves to do checkmates with all different combinations of pieces.

I couldn't analyze the board the way my dad did though.

He could look at the board and tell you what you should have done five moves back to win at the current point in the game. He could memorize the way the board looked throughout the whole game.

Sure, I could memorize the prescribed moves and theories for how the endgame 'should' go, and learn to trade pieces not pawns in the middle game. But I was never going to be as good as he was.

Eventually, I gave up on playing chess because of all the pressure to be as perfect as my dad, when clearly that was never going to happen.

The Pitfalls of Perfectionism

In so many ways, perfectionist parents kill their children's dreams before they even have a chance to be born.

Perfectionists take the joy out of childhood, by taking away children's fun and instead getting them to focus on the ideas of perfection. They punish and scold when something isn't 'good enough.' This can lead to a huge amount of stress for the child who is always trying to please their parents, and to depressed feelings when they can't measure up.

According to Dr. Jonice Webb (Running on Empty, Page 14),

You can imagine that when narcissists become parents they demand perfection from their children, or at the very least, no embar-

rassment. While healthy parents may cringe a little when their child fails to catch the fly ball in the big game, the narcissist parent of that child is angry and feels personally humiliated. When their children make mistakes that are visible to others - no matter how much they may need their parents' help at that time - narcissists take it person- ally and make their children pay.

This can lead children, especially very young children to a great deal of stress that they are ill-prepared to cope with. All the child is doing is internalizing the message that it isn't ok to make mistakes, because mistakes will be harshly punished. This instills fear in the child and takes away any opportunity to take meaningful learning from their mistakes.

Perfectionist parents teach their children that they are to be feared, as well as the punishers of the child's mistakes.

According to <u>Very Well Family</u>,

Perfectionist parenting, however, sets a child up to believe that if he doesn't achieve the highest standards, he's a failure. Putting too much pressure on kids to be perfect sends the wrong message. A child may cheat on his schoolwork to get good grades because he may think you value achievement over honest. Children of all ages need to be able to make mistakes without fear of major conse- quences, research shows, in order to learn.

Perfectionism can rub off on kids too. Kids who think they have to be perfect are at a higher risk of <u>mental health problems</u>, like de- pression, anxiety, and eating disorders. They're also good at hiding their symptoms so often their mental health problems go untreated.

Perfectionism doesn't help kids do better. In fact, it often makes them perform worse.

Having grown up in a family of perfectionists, I felt like I never belonged and like I would never be good enough to meet their expectations.

As a teen, I was diagnosed with depression. As an adult, I have also been diagnosed with Anxiety and PTSD. These conditions are partly due to growing up in a narcissistic, abusive and neglectful household. My parents also always expected me to be the best at everything and would withhold love based on achievements — or lack thereof.

No matter how well I did at anything, it was never enough.

When you live with a narcissist, their love is conditional. They don't love you just for being you, and that can be very damaging, especially for a child. With the perfectionistic narcissist, they will only show love to you based on achievements. This love is based on the image that you help to create for them.

If you do something that the narcissist can brag about to their friends, that will make them happy for a while. However, if you do something that displeases them, they are likely to become hostile towards you.

The Dark Side of Perfectionism

I remember being afraid of my parents from a very young age and trying to do my very best to please them all the time out of that fearfulness. I would start to feel anxious as soon as I walked in the door from school, because I never knew what kind of mood my dad would be in.

According to Science Daily,

The type of perfectionist who sets impossibly high standards for others has a bit of a dark side. They tend to be narcissistic, antisocial and to have an aggressive sense of humor. They care little about social norms and do not readily fit into the bigger social picture, a new article suggests.

The overlap between perfectionism and narcissism can create a toxic household for a child to grow up in. These kids don't really have the 'room' to just be kids. They must always be focused on achievement in order to please their parents. The focus on achievement forces them to grow up too quickly, instead of being able to play and make mistakes like normal kids.

When you live with a narcissistic perfectionist, they give you messages like, "It's my way or the highway," for example.

The narcissist doesn't acknowledge that there may be more than one right way to do something in any given situation. This teaches children blind obedience out of fear, instead of teaching problem solving and critical thinking skills.

The narcissistic parent sees the child as an extension of themselves. All they care about is how things in the family *look* from the outside, not how things *actually are*. Image is every-thing for them, and their *perfect children* are just an extension of that image.

According to Dalhouse University,

"A narcissistic perfectionist parent demands perfect performance from his daughter on the hockey rink, but not necessarily from any-one else out there," says Logan Nealis, a Clinical Psychology PhD student with the Personality Research Team. "They're getting a sense of vitality or self-esteem through the perfect performance of other people, and they bask in that glow vicariously."

When the child doesn't perform in a way that the parent thinks is up to par, they will guilt-trip and threaten the child to improve their performance. They will often make love contin-gent on performance. This hinders a child's normal development since they aren't receiving nurturing or any positive feedback from their parents on a consistent basis. Children need both positive and negative feedback from their parents to be able to thrive.

Letting Go of the Need for Perfection

Before he died, my dad apologized to me for his perfectionist ways when I was a child. He realized that he had pushed me too hard and damaged our relationship. He tried to make amends.

So, I know it is possible for a perfectionist to change. But do they have to be on their deathbed to do it?

Very Well Family suggests the following tips for parents to let go of perfectionism with their children:

1. *Consider your language.*
2. *Cut your child some slack.*
3. *Stay off the message boards and/or social media.*
4. *Focus on what you do right in parenting.*
5. *Send healthy messages about failure.*
6. *Pay attention to your child's efforts, not the outcome.*
7. *Back off when your child is overwhelmed.*

If you've been a perfectionist parent but you're able to dial it back a bit, don't sweat it too much — it's clear you're working hard to be the best parent you can be. And your willingness to acknowledge your weaknesses, learn from your mistakes, and cut yourself some slack will serve as a good role model for your child.

If however, you can't seem to let go of the idea that you need to be perfect or that your child needs to perform perfectly, consider seeking professional help. Sometimes, the quest for perfection stems from a mental health issue, like an anxiety disorder or a trauma history. At other times, perfectionism creates serious problems, like chronic stress or relationship difficulties.

Perfectionism can be damaging to both the perfectionist themself, and to their child. Unfortunately, the narcissistic types are the least likely to present for therapy, because the problem is always 'someone else's fault.' In the narcissist's mind, it is the fault of the child who has failed the parent by not being perfect at everything.

Chapter 5

Dynamics of Narcissistic Families

Were you the "black sheep" of your family? Did you have a sibling that could do no wrong? This fits the pattern of treatment common with narcissistic parents.

According to Dr. Jonice Webb (Running on Empty, Page 17):

When narcissists become parents, they are apt to have very different relationships with each of their children. They play favorites and often find at least one of their children a disappointment. But the one child who reflects them well, by being handsome or pretty or athletic or intelligent, is the "anointed one" and enjoys a special relationship with narcissist mommy or daddy. It is sometimes only in adulthood that the favored child of a narcissist realizes that her parent's love has been conditional all along.

In much of the research on narcissistic parents, the way the children are referred to is that one child is the "golden child" and the other is the "scapegoat." The golden child is the favorite, and the scapegoat is the outcast of the family.

In my family, my sister was the idolized golden child. Growing up, I used to refer to her as "the good child" and myself as "the bad child" because that is how our family always characterized us. This behavior by a narcissistic parent attempt to pit one child against the other, and the narcissist themself may have a special, and even positive relationship with their golden child.

One time my sister said to me, "Your experience of our family was very different from mine."

Of course, it was. She was the one that was treated well by our family, and to this day she is co-dependently enmeshed with my mother in ways that aren't normal for an adult. She relies on my mother for basic tasks, even though she is a smart adult with a child of her own.

According to Daughters of Narcissistic Mothers,

It's very common for Narcissistic Mothers to have a Golden Child and Scapegoat dynamic going on in their family.

What this means is this: one child in the family is the Golden Child, and one or more is the Scapegoat.

The Golden Child, as the name suggests, is the best and most wonderful child – at least in the eyes of the Narcissistic Mother. It seems to be that the Narcissistic Mother picks the Golden Child to be an extension of herself, onto whom she projects all her own supposed wonderfulness.

The Golden Child can do no wrong. She gets given the best of everything – perhaps even apartments or houses bought for her. Her most minor achievements are celebrated and held up for admiration. Her misdemeanours are glossed over and ignored.

The Scapegoat on the other hand is, also as the name suggests, the person on whom all the ills of the family are projected. They can do no right. Their major achievements are dismissed. Any money spent on them is the bare minimum and is spent begrudgingly.

The dynamic in my family wasn't unique. This type of golden child/ scapegoat relationship is common in many narcissistic families.

My relationship with my mother was always difficult. I knew that she didn't love me from a very young age, and as an adult

I questioned whether she even knew how to love. The problem was, I knew she loved my sister. She did things for my sister that she would never have done for me in a million years.

There were so many times that my mom helped my sister and prioritized her over me both in terms of time, love and finances. But the most poignant example for me is also the simplest.

One day my sister had gotten out of work and came over to my mom's house crying about how bad her day had been. I remember seeing my sister sitting there and crying, and my mother holding her while she cried, trying to reassure her.

My mother had never, ever held me while I cried. And there she was, the distant and non-feeling mother, holding my 30-something sister while she was crying.

My mother didn't tell my sister to suck it up. She didn't tell her that she had caused whatever problem she was facing. My mother was kind and empathetic.

But those feelings of kindness and empathy never extended to me. Not ever. I was always just, "the bad child."

That is what it is like to grow up in a family with narcissistic parents. The children are pitted against each other, and there may even be jealousy between the siblings. This can serve to fracture sibling relationships as well.

Daughters of Narcissistic Mothers Continues,

The Golden Child can end up very engulfed by the Narcissistic Mother, and her life can end up being enmeshed in the Narcissistic Mother's. She may well grow without proper boundaries and proper self-identity. She is likely to remain, either forever or for a long time, as a puppet of the Narcissistic Mother, and if she ever does manage to break free, that process will be infinitely more painful for her than it is for the Scapegoat.

The Scapegoat on the other hand, is the independent one. She's the one who's driven to seek answers and who may well realise about Narcissistic Personality Disorder. She's the one who can break free from the unhealthy dynamics of the family and do her best to create a healthy life and recover from the lies she was told about herself since the day she was born. It's still not easy for her (i.e. for you) of course. Nothing about this journey is easy. But it's doable, and possible.

It is interesting to note how the family dynamics carry forward into adulthood. The roles of golden child and scapegoat are usually well established in early childhood and will persist into adulthood as well.

If you are the scapegoat child, there is nothing that you can do to escape the role within the family. No amount of accomplishment will earn you forgiveness for your imagined wrongs against the family.

However, if you are the golden child like my sister, you will always maintain that role too. And no amount of screwing up is ever going to get you demoted from being the favorite.

The roles assigned by the narcissistic parent aren't always based on any innate qualities of the children themselves. It may have to do with the whims of the narcissist, or with their ideas of which child more closely resembles themselves in terms of temperament and other personality characteristics.

According to The Narcissistic Life,

Often the golden child is chosen for the role because they do actually possess some qualities or abilities that would reflect well on the narcissist. They may be the most attractive of their children, do well in school, or have some potential in a skill such as a sport or musical instrument. This is not always the case though, and sometimes the child who simply identifies the most strongly with the narcissistic parent will become the golden child.

In the case of my sister and I, she was the golden child almost from birth. This leaves me with a lifetime of questioning what I could possibly have done wrong by the time I was 3 years old to be chosen as persona non grata from such a tender age.

One of my earliest memories is of my mother leaving me alone to cry while she was rocking my sister to sleep as a baby. Instead of going into another room to play, I just sat in the hallway silently crying for a mother who didn't want me.

Since I was already exhibiting a trauma response to the situation in one of my earliest memories, it is some indication that I had been chosen already as the scapegoat child even before my sister was born. Of course, at 3 years old, there was no way that I could have understood that what I was exhibiting was an already ingrained trauma response. But looking back at the situation as an adult, I realize that conditioning had already taken place prior to that earliest memory. I was already traumatized at 3 years old, with no memory of what had gone on before.

My therapist asked me once if I had been a difficult baby, or if I had been sick a lot as a child. Although I have no memory of something like that, it is possible that a child with a difficult temperament or other issues would cause a narcissistic parent to dislike them almost immediately.

According to The Narcissistic Life the way the scapegoat child is treated can vary,

The nature and intensity of the abuse varies from family to family, depending on the type of narcissist we're talking about, and how severe their NPD is. Direct, overt verbal abuse such as insults, blaming, and put-downs are commonly reported, but in more extreme cases there may also be physical abuse.

My family was one such extreme case, as I was (albeit infrequently) abused by my dad. The first time my dad hit me as a teenager, because I couldn't make a pie crust of all things, my mother decided to come into my room and taunt me afterwards. Instead of trying to comfort me, or just leaving me alone to cry, she decided to come and yell at me and tell me that, "If you didn't make him mad, he wouldn't hit you."

Those words stuck with me for years and created a spiral of self-blame in my mind.

Oftentimes we internalize the negative messages that we get from our narcissistic families, because they begin from such a young age. We think that the things our parents tell us are true because we don't know any better. We think that the behaviors that go on in our homes are normal, because we have never known anything else.

According to The Narcissistic Life,

When we experience stress, neglect, and abuse early in life, it can have long-term effects on us. In one study of 21,000 people in Australia, those who experienced childhood abuse were at greater risk of poor mental health, particularly anxiety and depression, and poor physical health, including a higher risk of heart problems. The striking thing about this study, is that the participants were all over the age of 60. The researchers concluded that "the effects of childhood abuse appear to last a lifetime."

It is only when we become consciously aware that our parents are narcissists and that what they have said to us is not objectively true that we can begin to heal and make changes in our own lives.

Learning to recognize narcissistic abuse is crucial, so that we are able to distance ourselves from the negative messages of the narcissist. We need to realize that what they are saying isn't true, and that we deserve to be treated better. Sometimes this can take many years to realize, as these unhealthy patterns are the way we have lived our whole lives.

Chapter 6

The Covert Narcissist: A less obvious narcissist t

Sander Sammy on Unsplash

There are different types of narcissists, and the covert narcissist may be better at covering their tracks than what you would think of as a typical narcissist.

My mother is what you would think of as a covert narcissist. In the outside world, she seems like a sweet and caring person. She helps in her church and babysits other family member's kids.

However, inside the house, things were different. If things didn't go her way, she would become very manipulative. Often, she would play the victim to get what she wanted. She was the queen of guilt trips and gaslighting.

All of this is common behavior for a covert narcissist.

If you find yourself coping with someone who acts in this manner a large amount of the time, there is a high probability that you are dealing with a narcissist.

According to Psychology

There are criteria that are common to all narcissists, but with a covert narcissist, the behaviors may be more difficult to spot.

According to Very Well Mind,

In the field of psychology, behavior can be described as overt or covert. Overt behaviors are those that can be easily observed by others, such as those of the traditional narcissist described earlier. Covert behaviors, however, are those that are more subtle and a bit less obvious to others.

A covert narcissist is someone who craves admiration and importance as well as lacks empathy toward others but can act in a different way than an overt narcissist.

When considering the behavior of narcissists, it might be hard to imagine how someone could be a narcissist and be inhibited in their approach and behavior. A covert narcissist may be outwardly self-effacing or withdrawn in their approach, but the end goals are the same.

This was especially true with my mother. She was very focused on how our family appeared from the outside. That appearance was everything to her, and she cared more about how things looked to other people than our actual experiences as her children.

She didn't have a regard for our feelings or see us as individuals.

Narcissists see the people around them like cardboard cutouts. Paper dolls to be arranged 'just so.' They only see the surface level of other people, and don't bother getting to know them on deeper levels.

They might know things like your birthday or your favorite color. But they don't care about knowing the substance of your thoughts, feelings, or your life.

My mom would buy my sister and I matching clothes into our 30's even though we had very different styles. The only difference would be the color. Purple for me, and blue for my sister. What 30-year-old woman wants to dress in a matching outfit with her sister?

This is just a tiny illustration of the lack of depth that narcissists put to their relationships, but it can run even deeper. A narcissist won't care about your feelings at all and will probably never ask about them.

According to Very Well Mind, here are some signs of a covert narcissist:

Passive Self-Importance
Blaming and Shaming
Creating Confusion
Procrastination and Disregard
Giving With a Goal

Emotionally Neglectful

Giving with a goal is something that often happens in my family. People would give gifts—or money, they loved to give money—and use it like a chain around your neck. "I gave you money so you have to do what I want" was their slogan.

This isn't an overt manipulation like you would see with a more classic narcissist, but if you let them give you anything of value, a covert narcissist will hold it over your head for years!

Accepting help from them is the same. When they help, it is because they want to have free reign over controlling your life for an indefinite amount of time. Maybe forever.

Never ask a narcissist for help, and even if they offer, it is best for your mental health to decline!

What are Some Subtle Ways That a Covert Narcissist Abuses You?

Covert narcissists are the master manipulators

Covert narcissists are masters at manipulating things from behind the scenes and may seem like they are doing nothing at all if you aren't paying attention.

How Covert Narcissists Flip the Script

They thrive on tactics like gaslighting and playing the victim. Here is a closer look into some other ways that they can manipulate you.

According to Better Help,

Manipulation, gaslighting, and intimidation are all forms of abuse commonly used by covert narcissists. These tactics allow covert narcissists to systematically break down the people around them and to maintain a show of superiority. In overt narcissism, this show of superiority often comes in the form of loud boasts and attention-grabbing behavior. Still, in covert narcissism, the process is often less easy to recognize. Through putting themselves down, downplaying their talents, and continually twisting the story, covert narcissists cause severe trauma to others. If are a survivor of a covert narcissist's abuse, healing may take time and professional intervention. Whether you seek help from a counselor in your area or seek the help of an online therapist, such as those from BetterHelp, healing from covert narcissistic abuse is possible and reaching out for help is the first step.

When a narcissist gaslights you, as discussed earlier, this is the ultimate crazy-making. They will change the narrative around past events to their whims, and make you feel like your own memory of events may be faulty.

Similarly, when covert narcissists play the victim, they are twisting the narrative to make it seem like everything that has happened to create problems in the relationship is your fault.

Intimidation is another method that covert narcissists use to flip the script.

According to Better Help,

Intimidation tactics may be easy to see, as is the case when someone grows aggressive and confrontational. Intimidation does not have to be physical, though, and does not have to involve yelling or a physical altercation. Instead, intimidation by a narcissist might look far more akin to defensive lashing out. For instance, if a friend goes to a covert narcissist and says, "Hey. You mocked me in front of everyone yesterday, and I was upset by it. It was not an appropriate thing to do," the covert narcissist may then respond, "It was a joke! Can you not take a joke? I didn't know you were so sensitive." This tears the other person down, dismisses their frustration, and paints the narcissist as nothing more than an entertaining jokester who is just a little bit misunderstood.

The key thing that the narcissist is doing with manipulation, gaslighting and intimidation is changing the narrative around what happened to make themselves look good, and to make the victim look bad. Usually, the reverse is usually true.

Narcissists are great at making you doubt yourself and think that you are going crazy because you misinterpret situations. They want you to lose trust in yourself so that you will stay attached to them and they can control you even more.

Eventually, you will go around believing that everything bad that happens is your fault. This faulty belief can cause extremely low self-esteem in victims of narcissistic abuse, as well as a host of other emotional and psychological problems.

Chapter 7

Raised by a Narcissist

The suffering of having a narcissistic mother

Photo by <u>ariyan Dv</u> on <u>Unsplash</u>

Growing up, I tried to run away from home quite a few times. Mostly because I thought my parents didn't want me.

When I was 16, they shipped me off to live with my aunt and uncle in another town. I think they thought that my depression was "too much", and they didn't want to deal with it. They never once accepted any responsibility for being a partial cause of my depression through their treatment of me.

A lifetime of being the scapegoat child can take its toll on your mental health.

Years later, my mother decided to bring it up that I had run away from home as a teen out of nowhere at a family dinner. We were playing dominoes, then casually out of nowhere she said to me, "When you ran away from home, I didn't want you to come back. You only came back because your dad wanted that."

Even in my 30's, knowing that my mother didn't want me still hurt.

I think that being around the rest of her narcissistic family emboldened her to say terrible things to me, to impress them. Her whole side of the family is toxic, and I used to leave every family dinner in tears. That day was no different.

If you have a narcissist in your life, they get into the habit of saying horrible things to you for no reason. It isn't about us; it is about them. They like hurting people. At least that's what my therapist says.

Realizing that my mother liked to hurt people took me a long time, because so many people looking at our family from the outside used to say that she was the nicest person. This is how well a covert narcissist can play their role with the outside world.

When we were interacting with anyone else, it was accepted as a matter of course that I was the one in the family who was troubled, and that the rest of our perfect family was blameless.

The realization that my mother liked hurting people came to me in therapy.

During one of my sessions, I was talking about how I used to dread phone calls from my mother around the holidays. I had broken off contact with my toxic aunt and uncle before I stopped talking to my mother, because they were overtly hostile towards me.

Still, my mother used to invite me to my aunt and uncle's house for every holiday, trying to force us into some kind of contrived relationship that none of us wanted.

In one such call with my mother about Easter, I told my mom that I didn't want to go because my uncle was always mean to me.

She said, "But isn't it fun to say something mean back?"

My therapist really narrowed into that point. She said, "Your mother thinks that being mean is fun."

I had never thought about it that way before, and it really helped me to find some peace about the image that I had in my head of my mother being the nicest, most perfect person that everyone else thought that she was.

Growing up, my mom liked to tell me stories of things that she and her siblings had done as children. One of these stories also illustrates the idea that my mom liked being mean.

Apparently, my mom and her siblings used to swing their cat around by the tail and throw it to see if it landed on its feet. Putting that together with the idea that my mom liked to be mean made something click inside my mind. I knew from watching hundreds of episodes of Criminal Minds that hurting animals is a precursor to hurting people and can be a sign of being a sociopath.

According to <u>Narcissisms</u>,

More Machiavellian narcissists may be cruel to animals. Particularly when they're younger.

A friend of mine once had a game called "operation last supper". This is where he threw bread on his shed roof to feed the birds. What a lovely gesture. Then proceeded to shoot them with his air rifle.

The narcissists lack of emotional empathy extends to animals. So they don't feel their pain. And don't lie awake at night feeling guilty for the suffering they've caused. This makes it easier for them to mistreat animals.

The story of my mother and her siblings with the cat really fits this pattern of animal abuse as a precursor to abusing people in adulthood. For this reason, be wary of ever leaving a narcissist with your pet. They really don't care about animals the way that other people do.

Chapter 8

Recognizing a Narcissist

My Narcissistic Mother Lied to Me
And it took me a long time to realize how often

Photo by Pixabay

Since I didn't want to go to family get-togethers with my mother and the rest of her toxic extended family it got to the point where I learned to hold firm to my boundaries and kept saying no to her requests for attendance.

After a couple of years of this, my mom started inviting me to her house for holidays instead of to my aunt and uncle's house. I would ask her who was going. She would tell me, "Oh, just you and your sister." Ok. That was fine. So, I would tell her that I would go.

I would get to her house for the holiday event, then about an hour after I got there, more people would show up. People I had no idea were coming and had no desire to have contact with. They would walk in the door and, in place of a greeting, say something horrible to me.

Then, still holding my boundaries, I would leave.

After I caught onto the fact that she was lying to me when she invited me, and doing the whole "sneak inviting" thing, I stopped going to her house for any holiday.

You must hold firm boundaries with narcissists, because they don't respect you, and will lie and manipulate to get what they want.

Chapter 9

Growing up with a Narcissist

When you grow up with a narcissist for a parent, it is like you are always alone inside, but never alone outwardly.

What you think and feel is completely ignored. It is like you are a shell of a person. One dimensional. Like a puppet or a doll. You are just there to look pretty and perfect but never say or do anything.

In my generation, children were supposed to be seen and not heard.

When you learn that you can't speak, all your feelings are negatively directed inward. You become emotionally self-harming.

According to Psych Central, there are 5 Common Struggles Children of Narcissists Face in Adulthood:

They have people-pleasing tendencies.

They suffer from a persistent sense of self-doubt.

They feel guilt, shame, and fear about succeeding or being in the spotlight.

They have insecure or anxious attachment styles and often end up in abusive relationships as adults.

They feel defective and worthless.

Over the years, I have experienced all these things because of growing up with a narcissist. It has been difficult to overcome all these issues in adulthood, although therapy has helped a great deal, as has being in a healthy relationship.

If you have grown up with a narcissist, you may feel like you are to blame for being unloved. You may think that you aren't loveable at all. That isn't true.

Learning self-love can be a huge step towards healing, and I would highly recommend going to therapy to find out if you may have PTSD as well from your difficult childhood. A diagnosis and the resulting therapy are a huge steps towards healing, and can help make you feel validated instead of crazy.

Chapter 10

I Wasn't the First Person in my Family to go No-Co

It should have been a clue that something in our family was badly wrong.

When I was 8 or 10 years old, my aunt inexplicably stopped talking to everyone in our family. She didn't talk to any of us for years.

I remember, as a little girl, going to her apartment complex to go swimming, and we always had a good time. Then, with no explanation, those swimming days stopped. She didn't come to any holidays. My parents never told us why.

Then, years later, when my dad got cancer, he started apologizing to everyone that he felt he had wronged in his life. My aunt was on that list. He called and left her a voicemail. To everyone's surprise, she responded.

Generational Trauma

On my mom's side of the family, there is a lot of generational trauma. It goes back at least to my grandpa, maybe before.

When my Aunt started talking to our family again after she rejoined our family, she and I spent quite a bit of time together. She confided in me a lot about her growing up years, things that I had never heard from my mother or anyone else.

She stopped talking to our family because of her own history of trauma within the family.

Honestly, in terms of her mental health, maybe she would have been better off if she had never talked to us again. It had to be hard to see everyone again years later, when she clearly hadn't healed from all the pain and resentment of the past.

I know that she did some therapy but based on the reactions she had to dealing with our family, I don't think it was enough for her to feel ok about being back in contact.

That, and our family on my mom's side is toxic anyway. It couldn't have been easy for her.

It Should Have Been a Sign

Most normal people don't have family members that completely cut off contact from everyone else. Going no-contact is typically seen as a "nuclear option" to be considered only after other attempts at fixing family relationships have failed.

Our family never said why she had done it. They blamed it on her being crazy.

Although I didn't know it at the time, many therapists recommend cutting ties with toxic family members, even if it is immediate family. This is much more likely than my aunt just being "crazy." Most likely, a mental health professional had told her to cut off contact for the benefit of her mental health.

Family is a key factor in our lives. We depend on our families, spend time with them, and family relationships are often central to our lives into adulthood.

According to Very Well Family,

Cutting ties with family members is more common than you might think. It's just not often talked about. For some people, it might be embarrassing. Others fear sounding cruel. And many simply prefer to keep family issues private.

A 2015 U.S. study found that more than 40% of individuals have experienced family estrangement at one point in their lives. A U.K. study found that it affects at least one in five British families.

And while estrangement often encompasses extended family, it's fairly common in immediate families as well. Another U.S. study found that 10% of mothers are currently estranged from at least one adult child.

As someone who always had a tumultuous relationship with my family, the example of my aunt's estrangement from our family should have been a clue to me that my family is toxic. It should have been a clue that it wasn't just me. It should have felt validating, but it didn't.

Having someone else in my family cut everyone off for ten years should have been like a big, flashing, neon sign that something in our family was badly wrong. But it wasn't.

I still spent years afterward blaming myself for not being loved by my family, even though I wasn't the only black sheep on that side of the family.

My dad was the only one that I know of whoever apologized to my aunt for whatever was wrong with our family. Everyone else just treated her like a second-class citizen in our family. They took her back, but it was on their terms. None of them bothered to be any nicer to her. If anything, they treated her worse than before.

Her estrangement was used as an excuse for treating her as "less than" everyone else in the family. They held onto blame for her action of leaving, even though it is likely that she had acted out of self-preservation and not malice.

According to Psych Central,

People can change, but toxic people rarely do. They lack self-awareness and don't take responsibility for their actions. And since they don't see how their behavior hurts you, they refuse to change. Instead, they blame you and expect you to cater to their demands.

My family's behavior was fairly consistent with what the research discusses.

If your family is treating you badly, you may want to first try to have a talk with them about why they are treating you badly. Although if they are narcissists, it is unlikely that it will be a helpful conversation.

In any kind of normal family, they would likely apologize or at least calmly try to explain the behavior that is upsetting you. If they just get angry and try to blame you, odds are that you aren't dealing with simple family squabbles. It is likely that one or more of your family members is a narcissist, or at least has a narcissistic lack of empathy.

Normal families have good communication and can apologize for wrongs that are committed within the family, and to make amends.

If you are enmeshed in a toxic or narcissistic family, it is likely that you will at the very least need to set some firm boundaries with them to manage your mental health in the context of these relationships. Remember, your mental health needs to be a priority over your relationships, even family relationships.

Healthy relationships don't require you to sacrifice your well-being to participate in them. If you are consistently sacrificing your own mental and emotional health to cope with relationships, then they are toxic to you and need to be treated as such. It is perfectly ok to hold people at arm's length if they are actively hurting you and have a total disregard for the consequences of their behavior.

Chapter 11

How Early Relationships With Your Parents Can Affe

Do you struggle in relationships? This could be why.

Photo by Wix.

It is true that relationships aren't always perfect, yet they should be equitable and beneficial overall. If relationships are negative most of the time, or more than they are positive, it may be time to question if you are in the right kind of relationship.

You may have begun to realize that your parents were narcissists when you started having problems in your adult relationships. Often, we simply accept the way that we were parented as children, because we don't know another way is possible. This can sometimes lead to troubled romantic relationships in adulthood as well.

Since I didn't have the best relationships with my parents as a child, the lack of a secure attachment style in childhood is still affecting me today.

When you didn't have the perfect childhood, you may be carrying attachment issues into adulthood. Throughout my life, people I loved told me that they would always be there for me, but when the going got rough, they always ended up leaving. This created the belief that relationships aren't trustworthy, so I must prepare for the people I love to leave.

Often, when we have been raised by narcissists in childhood, we will attract unhealthy relationships in adulthood as well. So, if you have a narcissistic parent, it may be no surprise when you end up with a narcissistic adult partner as well. You have been raised to think that this type of relationship is normal.

Due to childhood issues, I didn't have a healthy relationship style in adulthood for many years. I alternated between feeling overly needy and pushing people away. This resulted in tumultuous relationships with my partners over the years.

If you had grown up in a household with healthy, loving parents, it is more likely that you would have a happy and healthy relationship with your partner and friends.

How we are raised in childhood, and our relationships with our parents, serve as the template for our other relationships later in life. Early relationships build the foundation for other relationships, and we form relationship patterns based on the relationships templates that we have experienced and observed in childhood.

What are attachment styles?

There are four different attachment styles, which bring about different types of relationships with our parents and other caregivers later in life.

According to The Attachment Project, the four attachment styles are:

1. *Anxious (also referred to as Preoccupied)*
2. *Avoidant (also referred to as Dismissive)*
3. *Disorganized (also referred to as Fearful-Avoidant)*
4. *Secure*

The goal of parenting is to help our children to form a **Secure Attachment** with us, which will in turn improve their relationships later in life. This can be done through using an Attachment or Authoritative Parenting approach . A secure attachment makes people well-adjusted and generally prepared with the skills to have happy relationships.

According to The Attachment Project,

"Adults with a secure attachment style can depend on their partners and in turn, let their partners rely on them.

Relationships are based on honesty, tolerance, and emotional closeness.

The secure attachment type thrive in their relationships, but also don't fear being on their own. They do not depend on the responsive-

ness or approval of their partners, and tend to have a positive view of themselves and others."

I am at the other end of the spectrum with a **Disorganized Attachment.** This can be a result of parenting that is either abusive, neglectful, or both. When children aren't parented in a loving way, then they haven't learned the skills necessary to have healthy relationships later in life.

Relationships have not always been easy for me. According to the <u>Personal Development School</u>, for those with a disorganized attachment style,

Relationships "can feel **chaotic, confusing and overwhelming** *because you swing between being avoidant and anxious.*

This can be incredibly painful for both you and your romantic partners — as depending on the relationship, your mental state can shift from: "I want you... come closer!" to "Slow down, not THAT close!"

If you're dating someone more avoidant, you may become "needy," insecure or anxious because **you fear abandonment**.

Or, on the other end of the spectrum, if you're dating someone who is more anxiously attached, you might become more avoidant and even feel turned off when they get too close."

A disorganized attachment style has made it difficult for me to maintain close relationships, because I am constantly afraid that love isn't going to last. When I perceive someone as threatening, or not meeting my needs in some way, I push them away. But, if someone is too needy, it is exhausting and I pull away instead.

In between the Secure and Disorganized Attachment Styles are Anxious / Preoccupied and Avoidant / Dismissive.

According to <u>The Attachment Project</u>, people with an **Avoidant/ Dismissive** Attachment style typically will not need to be in a relationship, and have a tendency to avoid closeness.

"The dismissing / avoidant type tend to believe that they don't have to be in a relationship to feel complete.

They do not want to depend on others, have others depend on them, or seek support and approval in social bonds.

Adults with this attachment style generally avoid emotional closeness. They also tend to hide or suppress their feelings when faced with a potentially emotion-dense situation."

On the other hand, people with an **Anxious / Preoccupied Attachment** style are obsessed with their relationships. They are always thinking about their partner, their partner's needs, and what their partner thinks of them. According to The Attachment Project, "

"The anxious adult often seeks approval, support, and responsiveness from their partner.

People with this attachment style value their relationships highly, but are often anxious and worried that their loved one is not as invested in the relationship as they are.

A strong fear of abandonment is present, and safety is a priority. The attention, care, and responsiveness of the partner appears to be the 'remedy' for anxiety.

On the other hand, the absence of support and intimacy can lead the anxious / preoccupied type to become more clinging and demanding, preoccupied with the relationship, and desperate for love."

After reading through these different attachment styles, it is easy to see how any of the insecure attachment styles would potentially alienate a partner in relationships. This is especially true if both partners have any style other than secure attachment. If that is the case for you in your current relationship, it will be beneficial to work on communication skills or consider going to relationship counseling.

To determine your attachment style, you can also take an <u>attachment styles quiz</u>.

Although reading about attachment issues may give you a bleak outlook on your current relationship or possible future relationships, don't lose heart. Similarly, to how childhood relationships shape our adult attachment styles, a secure relationship in adulthood can also serve to heal childhood attachment issues.

There are ways to work through your attachment issues and overcome them in adulthood; the key thing is bringing these patterns into your conscious awareness so that you can change them. When we are unaware of our unhealthy relationship patterns, we just keep repeating them over and over. Once these patterns become conscious, then there are conscious actions that we can take to change them as well.

Chapter 12

Are You Suffering from Childhood Emotional Neglect

When children are young, they form bonds of attachment with parents and other caregivers, as discussed in the previous chapter. A key component of attachment is Emotional Responsiveness. This means that a caregiver responds to the child's emotional needs in a responsive manner.

But what about when children's emotional needs aren't met?

This can lead to a condition referred to as **Childhood Emotional Neglect**. Now, this doesn't always mean that a child has been physically abused or neglected, it is their feelings that have been ignored repeatedly throughout childhood.

According to Healthline,

Childhood emotional neglect occurs when a child's parent or parents fail to respond adequately to their child's emotional needs. Emotional neglect is not necessarily childhood emotional abuse. Abuse is often intentional; it's a purposeful choice to act in a way that is harmful. While emotional neglect can be an intentional disregard for a child's feelings, it can also be failure to act or notice a child's emotional needs. Parents who emotionally neglect their chil-

dren may still provide care and necessities. They just miss out on or mishandle this one key area of support.

Many times, parents are loving and well-meaning, and still manage to emotionally neglect their children. However, with children of narcissists, this may not be the case. The narcissist is self-absorbed and may neglect the child just because they don't think of feelings as being important. Other times, neglect can be intentional and more malignant. There will be narcissistic parents that are on both ends of the spectrum.

According to The New England Psychologist,

The largest part are the WMBNT group: "well-meaning but neglected themselves." Mostly, these parents really they love their children. They give their children everything except emotional attunement because they don't have it themselves. It is an emotional blind spot that gets passed on from one generation to another.

This describes emotional neglect passing down through generations, similarly to the way that generational trauma was discussed previously. Parents neglect their children's emotions because that is what they learned growing up from their own parents.

People are likely to parent in the same way that their parents did with them, since this is what they know. It takes very intentional actions to break out of this type of cycle.

Feelings are hard and scary to talk about, so oftentimes in families, and in society, we fail to talk about them. This can lead to people growing up with a big, gaping, empty hole inside where their feelings are supposed to be. That empty hole is caused by Childhood Emotional Neglect.

So, what does Childhood Emotional Neglect look like?

According to Dr. Jonice Webb (Running on Empty) some symptoms of Childhood Emotional Neglect are:

1. *Feelings of Emptiness*

2. *Counter-Dependence*
3. *Unrealistic Self-Appraisal*
4. *No Compassion for Self, Plenty for Others*
5. *Guilt and Shame*
6. *Self-Directed Anger, Self Blame*
7. *The Fatal Flaw (If People Really Knew Me, They Won't Like Me)*
8. *Difficulty Nurturing Self and Others*
9. *Poor Self-Discipline*
10. *Alexithymia*

If any of these sound like you, then you may be suffering from Childhood Emotional Neglect as the result of growing up with a narcissist.

You are probably looking at the word Alexithymia and asking yourself what that means, as it is not a common word in our English lexicon. **Alexithymia is a psychological term that means to be out of touch with your feelings.** This is a common occurrence when you grow up with a narcissist who always uses your feelings as ammunition against you.

When growing up with a narcissist, you may have spent years developing the coping mechanism of stuffing your feelings down as far as possible and trying not to feel them at all. It can help you survive living with a narcissist but may cause a lot of struggles for you later in life.

According to Dr. Jonice Webb (Running on Empty, page 98),

Alexithymia denotes a person's deficiency in, knowledge about, and awareness of emotion. In its extreme form, the alexithymic is a person for whom feelings are indecipherable; both their own and other people's. The alexithymic lives his life with no willingness or ability to tolerate, or even experience, emotions. I have observed that many people with alexithymia have a tendency to be irritable. They tend to snap at others for seemingly no reason, and it obviously in-

terferes with their relationships. It allows them to hold others at a distance, even as it leaves them terribly alone.

Just as we develop attachment issues from coping with narcissistic parents, we also learn unhealthy ways of dealing with our own feelings. When you have a narcissistic parent, their feelings are often the only feelings that matter. You learn from a very young age that your feelings don't matter, or that your feelings are a burden or a nuisance. This can result in unhealthy ways of coping with your feelings that last into adulthood.

If we don't learn to manage our feelings in childhood, we will need to learn to do so in adulthood, or we will have chronic problems with relationships and perhaps with friends and at work also. Feelings permeate every aspect of our lives and being inept at coping with them can lead to a whole host of problems.

To cope with problems managing our feelings, we first need to learn basic skills that we should have learned in childhood. We need to learn to allow ourselves to feel our feelings, to name them, and to develop coping skills for when we feel upset. We also have the added layer of coping with blame and shame around just allowing ourselves to feel our feelings, in addition to the skills that other people need to learn who haven't been abused or neglected.

As we work to heal from narcissistic abuse in adulthood, coping with feelings is a major skill that we will have to learn. This can be done in the context of adult relationships, as well as with a therapist.

Narcissistic Relationships

Chapter 13

Dealing With a Narcissist

In some situations, you may either not wish to cut off contact with a narcissist, or not be able to. An example of this would be when you must co-parent with a narcissist. Also, sometimes you don't feel ready to cut off contact completely with a family member and want to try less drastic tactics first.

When you are dealing with a narcissist, there are several ways to handle interactions with them, to lessen the distress that they are likely to cause you. It is important to manage all your interactions carefully, so that you don't give them more ammunition to throw back at you at a later time.

Narcissists love to keep track mentally of all the things that you have 'done wrong' so it is important to let them perceive you as being as boring as possible. That way, they have nothing to blame or shame you for. This takes away a portion of their power against you.

Here are some helpful ways that you can deal with the narcissist in your life.

GRAY ROCK TECHNIQUE

The Gray Rock technique is commonly recommended for dealing with a narcissist, if there isn't a way for you to break off contact with them.

According to **Better Up,**

Grey rocking is a technique used to divert a toxic person's behavior by acting as unresponsive as possible when you're interacting with them. For example, using the gray rock method involves deliberate actions like avoiding eye contact or not showing emotions during a conversation.

When you do have to interact with the narcissist, give them as little attention as possible. Answer questions simply, and don't give out any personal information about yourself, as this can be used against you later as ammunition. Give one- or two-word answers to questions if at all possible. Don't ask them any questions.

As you give the narcissist short answers, it makes the interaction less rewarding for them. Similarly, when you don't ask for any information about their lives, it lets them know that you find them to be uninteresting as well. These techniques can take away their power in the relationship, as contact becomes less and less emotionally charged.

When you Gray Rock, basically, you are making each interaction as short and boring as possible to show the narcissist that you aren't willing to engage with their manipulative tactics. There is no new information that you are giving them that allows them to manipulate you further.

According to Better Up,

The idea behind this technique is that toxic people feed on your reaction. A narcissistic coworker, for example, feeds on conflict, drama, and attention.

By making yourself and your interactions with them as neutral as possible, they'll eventually lose interest. Your lack of response will have them looking for someone else to target and project onto. Or, ideally, give up the damaging behavior.

Grey rocking is a strategy that some <u>mental health professionals</u> recommend to clients who have a toxic person in their life.

According to Nadene van der Linden, a clinical psychologist at the Massachusetts Association for Psychoanalytic Psychology, <u>the grey rocking technique can be used in response to abusive, control-ling, and manipulative behaviors</u>. Van der Linden teaches her clients how to use it appropriately when they deal with negative <u>behaviors</u>.

The Gray Rock technique can be useful in all different types of situations, such as responding to gaslighting, manipulation, and overt insults. When you use the Gray Rock technique, you will learn to respond in a non-threatening and non-reactive way. By doing so, it gives the narcissist nothing to latch onto in the conversation as fuel for their insults.

You can simply give yes or no, or other one-word answers to questions. If this isn't possible, at least give as little personal information as possible. If they persist in asking questions that you aren't comfortable answering, simply tell them that you are not willing to answer. Enforce firm boundaries in the conversation. Be brief and to the point. Move on from the conversation as quickly as possible.

SETTING BOUNDARIES.

If you have family members that you think may be narcissists, it is very important to <u>set boundaries</u> with them. Boundaries are important because of the narcissist's codependency, and their desire to control your life as much as possible.

My mom always wanted my sister and I to come over for dinner at her house every night, even as adults with children of our own. At a certain point, this wasn't feasible for me anymore. I lived half an hour away, I had a new baby, and we only had one car. That meant, to have dinner with her after work, it took me

1.5 hours to travel just to come and see her. That wasn't something I could do every day. When I told her this, she was angry and dismissive, and told me that my sister did it for her and I should too.

Narcissists are likely not to accept your boundaries. When I tried to talk to my mom about setting a boundary with her, she told me to my face that I didn't deserve to have boundaries.

That just made me put up stronger boundaries, to keep her farther and farther out of my family and our day-to-day lives. Sticking up for yourself is extremely important and should be non-negotiable.

When you begin to set boundaries with a narcissist, they are likely to become angry and hostile, and will often push back against your boundaries. Setting boundaries makes the narcissist angry because they know that it is a sign that they have lost control over you. Often, they will attempt to get you back under their control.

According to Talkspace,

Setting firm boundaries with somebody who has narcissistic personality disorder may trigger them into cycling through their behavior. Be prepared for them to:

- *Act like a victim*
- *Argue with you*
- *Blame you or make things seem like your fault*
- *Accuse you of being too sensitive*
- *Minimize your feelings*
- *Become angry*

The bottom line, and what you must keep in mind, is that your boundaries need to be put in place. You're taking care of yourself, and you deserve to have boundaries in place that protect you and make you feel safe and comfortable in your relationship.

You may tell the narcissist, "If you are hostile and belittling to me on the phone, I am going to hang up with you." If you do this, be sure to follow through. Otherwise, a narcissist will continue to violate your boundaries in the future.

If you are seeing the narcissist in person, you can also make it clear that you will leave immediately if your boundary is violated. This may sound harsh but realize that their mistreatment of you all this time has also been harsh. You are taking a firm stance against behavior that is intolerable.

According to Talkspace, here are some of the types of boundaries that you should set with a narcissist:

- *Don't let them talk to you any way that they want*
- *Don't let them treat you in a disrespectful or hurtful manner*
- *Ask them not to share personal information with others*
- *Demand they respect your opinions and thoughts*
- *Insist that they listen when you say "no"*
- *Ask for your personal space when you need it*
- *Make sure that you are OK with the physical and sexual aspects of the relationship*
- *Ensure that your financial relationship is equitable and acceptable*

When you set boundaries, it is important to do so in a firm but kind manner. Don't let the narcissist visibly upset you when you are trying to hold a boundary. Remember to hold firm and leave the situation immediately if a boundary has been violated.

Limited Contact

When you are in the process of setting boundaries with a narcissist, it may be helpful for your mental health to limit the amount of contact that you have with them. This allows you to mentally protect yourself from the constant onslaught of their narcissistic behaviors.

According to The Narcissistic Life,

It might be worth considering going low contact with your Narcissistic mother if:

- *You continue to feel disrespected by your mother.*
- *Your relationship with your mother is negatively impacting other relationships in your life.*
- *Your mother uses sensitive information you tell her against you.*
- *You feel smothered or overwhelmed by your mother.*
- *You feel a constant sense of dread and angst because of your mother.*
- *You continue to tolerate emotional abuse.*

Ongoing emotional, physical or financial abuse can take a huge toll on your mental health. If the constant crazy-making and abuse is becoming too much for you to handle on a regular basis, then limited contact may be a good solution for you.

You may decide that you will only see the narcissist on certain occasions, in controlled or public environments, or that you will only talk on the phone or via email.

According to The Narcissistic Life,

Sometimes, it's not practical (or even desirable) to avoid all contact with your mother. For instance, you may live with her.

Or, you may have a tight-knit family, and a no contact approach might strain or disrupt the cherished relationships you share with others.

Moreover, you might simply want to have a relationship with your mother. Even if you know that it won't resemble the stereotypical parent-child dynamic, there's nothing wrong with wanting to have your mother in your life.

Finally, some people hope to cut contact with their mothers- at some point. Going low contact with your narcissistic mother acts somewhat like a trial run.

You can see how it feels to reduce your communication and closeness to determine if you want to continue moving forward with your decision.

When you choose to limit contact with a narcissist, this can give you some peace of mind, and personal space. This time apart can give you time to collect your thoughts and focus on your healing, and other positive aspects of your life.

Limited contact can go on for a specific amount of time, or this may be your approach to dealing with a narcissist indefinitely. The choice is yours.

How much you decide to limit contact with a narcissist won't just depend on what has happened in the past, but also on how much of a constant source of stress that they are in your life. Limited contact can look different for everyone, depending on numerous factors in the relationship that you have with the narcissist, as well as other family members.Narcissistic Relationships

Chapter 14

What are the Phases of Narcissistic Abuse?

And why is it so hard to break away from a relationship with a narcissist.

When you first meet a narcissist, they often reel you in because of how charismatic they are. They seem to be the life of the party, and they shower you with attention.

They seem so fun and exciting to be around, and so interested in you, that you are already hooked on the relationship from the beginning. So, when things start to go wrong, you question whether it is really in your head, and you should give them another chance.

Phases of Abuse

Narcissistic abuse comes in phases, it doesn't start all at once. Otherwise, there would be no reason for you to stay in this type of relationship. Things aren't bad right at the beginning. In fact, they are often extremely good.

According to Choosing Therapy,

The narcissistic abuse cycle is a pattern of highs and lows in which the narcissist confuses their partner through manipulation and calculated behaviors aimed at making their partner question themselves. The cycle has three specific phases: Idealization, devaluation, and rejection. Each works in tandem with the other in order to keep someone entangled in the narcissist's web.

As I mentioned earlier, often a relationship with a narcissist will be very good, almost intoxicating, at the beginning. Sometimes this is referred to as the honeymoon phase in a relationship. In psychology, it is called **Idealization**.

At the beginning of a relationship with a narcissist, they will be doing their best to make you feel special, loved, and wanted. Perhaps even more so than in a normal relationship. You may feel swept up in a rush of pleasant emotions, and the narcissist will likely take time to make you feel very special as well.

Here are some facets of what **Idealization** may look like, according to Choosing Therapy:

Love-bombing
A lot of attention given to partner
Grandiose gestures
Elaborate gifts and dates
Discussing marriage
Lack of boundaries

Attempts to isolate partner in the name of love
Quickly moving into intimacy
Creates a sense of ownership of partner and the relationship

When I first started dating my ex (the narcissist), he was very sweet and friendly. We would talk all the time. He even brought me a fancy dinner at work when I was working the night shift. Narcissists are great at sweet-talking to you, and making you think that they are deeply in love with you. This is what is commonly referred to as **Love Bombing**.

When a narcissist is love bombing you, they will likely go out of their way to do nice things with you that may seem out of proportion to the early stages of a typical relationship. This can include expensive gifts, nights out on the town, or taking you on nice trips. All of these may come as a surprise to you at the beginning of a relationship.

It doesn't take long for a narcissist to convince a partner that they are deeply in love with them, and for a partner to begin to return those feelings.

The next step of the cycle is called **Devaluation**. This is where things in the relationship begin to go badly wrong. In the case of my ex, right after we moved in together, he started cheating on me.

According to Choosing Therapy, the Devaluation stage may consist of some or all of the following behaviors:

Attempting to change their partner
Increasing criticism and insults
Gaslighting
Physical threats
Poor communication
Increased violation of boundaries
Triangulation
More isolation or control over their partner
Withholding physical, emotional, and sexual intimacy

You start to wonder, "what did I do wrong?" Things have gotten out of control, and often this will happen quickly. Since your partner was previously so sweet and was doting on you, it can make you question your own sanity when suddenly this split personality emerges.

It is like you are dating a completely different person. One that is constantly angry and mean.

Depending on how many times you have gone through this cycle with your partner, the devaluation stage can get progressively more volatile each time. Your partner may seem angrier and angrier with you, and nothing that you do to try to placate them seems to fix any of the problems.

Finally, the last stage of the narcissistic abuse cycle is **Rejection**. A lot of times, the narcissist will tell you that they are going to break up with you, or will break up with you, in yet another attempt at manipulation.

According to Choosing Therapy,

The rejection phase may include these types of behaviors:

Feelings of contempt and rage

Betraying the relationship

Invalidating their partner's emotions and placing all the blame on them

Playing the victim

Physical, emotional, and verbal abuse

Ending the relationship permanently or temporarily with attempts to continue this cycle of abuse

I experienced all these things with my ex too. When the narcissist finally has devalued you to your lowest point, they will try to kick you down even further. Sometimes going as far as physical abuse. This is a dangerous time for the victim of narcissistic abuse.

Once they do break up with you though, or you break up with them, the narcissist will often revert back to the honeymoon phase again and try to apologize and reel you back into the relationship. They will start back up with all the love-bombing all over again.

According to Choosing Therapy,

Second chances never work with narcissists. If they feel they are going to lose you from their life, the narcissist will do what they need to do to ensure you stick around and fall right back into the same habits. They will put on a show for a while until you are convinced that giving a second chance is worth the risk, then you will fall right back into the same cycle of psychological abuse.

The cycle of abuse can be repeated as many times as you let it, sometimes for years. A narcissist is going to attempt to control you for as long as they possibly can. They thrive off power and control.

Chapter 15

Why Does a Narcissist Treat Their Partner So Badly

Narcissists brains are wired differently than ours

If you are, or ever have been, in a relationship with a narcissist, you probably ask yourself frequently why they treat you so badly. You may wonder what you have done wrong to warrant this type of treatment.

The answer is nothing. You have done nothing wrong.

A narcissist's brain is wired differently than ours, and they don't think of relationships in the same terms that other people do. To them, a relationship is all about power and control.

As we discussed earlier, people commonly referred to as narcissists suffer from what is called, in Psychology, Narcissistic Personality Disorder. Since they have a psychological disorder that clouds their thinking, they are unable to have normal, caring relationships with other people. There always must be 'something in it' for them.

How Narcissists Think About Relationships

Most of us enter relationships wanting mutual love, affection and commitment. Not so for the narcissist.

According to Psych Central,

People with narcissistic personality disorder (NPD) have traits that are in opposition with the ability to love another person, at least in the way that people without NPD understand love. These traits include a lack of empathy, a sense of entitlement, and a tendency to exploit others for personal gain.

Narcissists look at other people as a means to an end. They don't look at others in an objective way, instead, they just look at what they would be able to gain from another person.

Psych Central Continues,

Narcissists may show you love and act in loving ways, but this tends to be conditional, in that displays of love depend on what you can give them in return. For people with NPD, relationships tend to be transactional.

Love is never going to be unconditional or equal with a narcissist because they don't love in the same way that normal people do. Narcissists tend to look at other people as though they are possessions. So, for them having a partner is about enhancing their personal image.

According to Psychology Today,

Narcissists tend to be attracted to trophy partners who are high in physical attractiveness or status. They are also well-known for their lack of commitment to partners, game-playing, and tendency to be on the lookout for a better partner.

Narcissists don't really love you, they don't even love the idea of being with you for the reasons that you may think. It isn't about companionship for them, it is all about what you can do for them on a material level, as well as for their self-image.

The Honeymoon Phase has Worn Off

Once the honeymoon phase of the relationship with a narcissist has worn off, then they will begin to treat their partner badly. Perhaps, they are tired of the relationship, or on the lookout for a better relationship. They may no longer be getting the adoration from the partner that was so gratifying for them early on.

Narcissists are also known for cheating on their partners.

According to Psych Alive,

When you are in a narcissistic relationship, you may feel very lonely. You might feel like you are just an accessory and your needs and wants are unimportant. Narcissistic partners act as if they are always right, that they know better and that their partner is wrong or incompetent. This often leaves the other person in the relationship either angry and trying to defend themselves or identifying with this negative self-image and feeling badly about themselves.

Once the narcissist has 'won' a potential mate, they will often grow bored with the relationship as the initial thrill wears off. This can lead the partner of a narcissist left to wonder what happened to the charming person that they fell in love with.

If you are noticing this taking place in your relationship, you may have also noticed other narcissistic and self-centered traits in your partner. If this is the case, you will want to extricate yourself from this relationship as quickly as possible.

Relationships with narcissists will just keep going downhill. Once the initial thrill wears off, the relationship will go into phases called Devaluation and Rejection. As this happens, the narcissist will continue to treat their partners (or, children and other family members) worse and worse.

Some common themes to narcissistic relationship behavior include manipulation, insults, gaslighting, and playing the victim; similarly to the behavior of narcissistic parents described in earlier chapters.

At times, when a narcissist gets to the rejection phase of a relationship, they can even become physically violent.

It is best to leave the relationship before it comes to this point, as it can be very dangerous attempting to leave a violent relationship.

Chapter 16

Leaving an Abusive Relationship

Make sure you have a safety plan in place, when you leave you are in more danger.

Photo by Pixabay

Being in an abusive relationship is terrifying. When someone you loved hurts you, it is like the ultimate betrayal.

People always ask survivors why they didn't leave sooner. The problem is people don't understand the fear that survivors face in abusive relationships. They haven't had the threats of, "If you leave again, I'm going to kill you!" screamed into their faces.

According to a story in the Clarion Ledger,

"The statistics are that women in abusive relationships are about 500 many times more at risk when they leave," said Wendy Mahoney, executive director for the Mississippi Coalition Against Domestic Violence. "Domestic violence is all about power and control, and when a woman leaves, a man has lost his power and control."

When you try to leave, an abuser will use threats to try to reel you back in. If the threats don't work, they will try to apologize and promise to change. If that doesn't work, then they will try to guilt trip or blackmail you. They try to wear down what little resolve you have, and make you feel like you are totally dependent on them.

After I left my abuser, I experienced this first-hand.

It wasn't the first time that I left, but it would be the last. He used my daughter to try to guilt trip me into staying. That had worked the time before. When it didn't work that time, he tried to trap me in the house. When I tried to run, he threw me down a flight of stairs.

I ran to the police station. I showed them the bruises where he choked me. I filed a police report.

I was still afraid; I had never filed a police report before.

If this sounds like your experience, then you are likely coping with domestic violence in addition to narcissistic abuse. In some extreme cases, narcissists do resort to physical violence when their threats and manipulation are not working with their partners anymore.

I was ill-prepared for my relationship to turn violent, and my whole life was wrapped up with my ex. I didn't know how to extricate myself from an increasingly more abusive relationship, so every time he would beg me to stay and give things another chance, I did. I didn't know what else to do.

Here are some tips for when you decide to leave an abusive relationship that I wish I would have known before trying to leave mine.

Creating a safety plan

When you are thinking about leaving an abusive relationship, it is important to plan ahead and create what is called a Safety Plan.

According to the National Domestic Violence Hotline,

A safety plan is a set of actions that can help lower your risk of being hurt by your partner. It includes information specific to you and your life that will increase your safety at school, home, and other places that you go on a daily basis.

Making a safety plan can include having a "go bag" ready for when you decide to leave. You may also want to stock away money or important documents like your identification and medical cards.

You can store these items at your office, or with a trusted friend or relative in preparation for leaving your abuser.

One of the most important things to keep in mind is that you will want to keep your plans primarily to yourself. If your abuser finds out that you are planning to leave, they may become more dangerous and violent. When you access any resources related to domestic violence, be sure that you are doing so from a private computer, so that

your abuser won't have access to your browsing history.

Despite the best of intentions, in some situations planning to leave the relationship may not be possible. *It is important to weigh the risks of staying in the relationship against leaving.* That is why I highlighted earlier in this chapter the dangers of leaving a violent relationship.

Many people will tell you that it is best to leave a violent relationship.

Only you can know for sure. There are many risk factors to be aware of before you leave, and it is a big decision that only you can make. It is important to weigh the pros and cons carefully, as you work on making this intensely personal decision.

According to <u>Domestic Shelters,</u>

Carlson recommends taking caution when leaving a relationship if your partner showed any signs of controlling behavior, including financial abuse, sexual coercion, isolating you from loved ones, verbal abuse and <u>gaslighting.</u>

"If you're dealing with any of this, it's best to talk to someone who has expertise in safety planning and the resources to get you the help you need," Carlson says. "Call a hotline or reach out to a shelter to talk to someone who can coach you through all the mechanisms you can use to leave safely."

Enlisting help is very important to getting away from a violent relationship.

I understand all too well the pain and shame of admitting that you have stayed in an abusive relationship. It is difficult to reach out for help because there is so much victim blaming in society as a whole. There are many reasons for victim blaming, but please know that being abused is not your fault. It is something that has happened to you, it is no reflection on who you are as a person.

If you have been in an abusive relationship with a narcissist, this is due to their own narcissistic tendencies, and the relationship has likely become abusive for reasons out of your control. Or, perhaps you have attempted to set boundaries to protect your mental well-being, and this has caused them to become violent.

Whatever the case, please don't blame yourself for your partner's abuse. They will try to make you feel like things are your fault, but this is an extreme manipulation tactic that they use to try to keep you under their control. The narcissist knows that the more you blame yourself for the abuse, the less likely it is that you will try to leave the relationship.

Here are some additional resources that will help you in making a Safety Plan.

If you are currently in an abusive relationship, you can reach out for help.

National Domestic Violence Hotline
Hours: 24/7. Languages: English, Spanish and 200+ through interpretation service
Learn more
800–799–7233

The best thing that someone did for me when I left my abuser was to take away my phone. That way, I wouldn't break down because of the incessant harassing and threatening phone calls and go back.

You may also be worried about other loved ones or pets and will want to get them away from the abuser safely as well. Planning for this can require a great deal of help and resources.

If you want to remove their pets or belongings from a mutual home, in the United States they can ask the police for what is called a Civil Standby.

A civil standby is a situation wherein an officer is present at the request of a party to a civil dispute in order to prevent violence. A civil assist is one in which officer merely monitors a scene to ensure the peace is kept, the officer's function in this situation being to stand by in the event trouble ensues with alleged victim — friends of the victim or family members.

The laws on Civil Standby will vary by state, so it is important to look up the laws for your state, or to call the police non-emergency number to find out what services they are able to provide.

Having a law enforcement officer present can help someone leaving a violent relationship to feel safe while they are collecting their pets or belongings.

Is Narcissistic Abuse a Crime?

Photo by <u>John Cameron</u> on <u>Unsplash</u>

Although it may feel like a crime has been committed against you when you are leaving a relationship with a narcissist, what will happen in the eyes of the law will depend on your specific circumstances.

If you have been a victim of domestic violence, that is likely one of the times that you will be able to file criminal charges against a narcissist. Other cases would be if they have destroyed or stolen your property, as well as documented ongoing stalking and harassment.

According to the University of South Florida,

"Domestic violence" means any assault, aggravated assault, battery, aggravated battery, sexual assault, sexual battery, stalking, aggravated stalking, kidnapping, false imprisonment, or any criminal offense resulting in physical injury or death of one family or household member by another family or household member.

If you have been a victim of any of these types of crimes, you may wish to consult with a lawyer, or file a police report.

The laws having to do with domestic violence in every state and country are somewhat different, so it can be important to research the laws for your location prior to filing a police report, unless you are currently in fear of your safety. In that case, you will want to contact the police immediately, and attempt to secure a restraining order, or protection order.

Getting Your Life Back

Filing charges against an abuser may feel like a way to punish them for what has happened, or to get your life back. It is a way to stand up against them and send the message that you will not tolerate the violence any longer. This is a decision to consider carefully, and with your support system in place.

It may take time for the case to proceed, and it is a good idea to get help from a Victim's Advocate as your case proceeds. They will be able to assist you through the process and explain the laws and procedures in your area. If you are not assigned an advocate by the court, you can ask for one.

Filing charges may not always lead to closure, but when you do, you are standing up not only for yourself, but for others who have been abused as well.

You May Never Get Justice or Closure

I didn't.

When I charged my ex with domestic violence he was found not guilty in the courts. It was a horrible experience, probably one of the worst days of my life, if not the actual worst.

He told the court that he hit me because I deserved it, and they let him go.

Now, this isn't the typical argument in a domestic violence court.

I don't want to make you panic. Many domestic violence cases will end with the abuser behind bars, or you with a restraining order against them, although mine didn't end that way.

However, this is also the reason that I advise consulting with either a lawyer or a victim's advocate if you are filing charges for domestic violence, because I didn't have access to either. I'm sure the prosecuting attorney was overworked, and I was only able to meet with him on one occasion.

This is also an important reason to have as much evidence as possible before you file charges for domestic violence. Otherwise, it just comes down to a he-said, she-said in court, and it will depend on who the jury finds to be more believable.

If you have any emails, text messages, social media posts, pictures of bodily or property damage, or any other evidence, make sure that you take it with you when you go to file the initial police report. That way, you will be sure to get all your evidence included in your case.

Even though I didn't win my case, I'm not sorry that I took my ex to court for domestic violence. It was important for me to tell my story on the stand, look him in the eye, and let him know that I wasn't going to be intimidated by him anymore.

Also, having a restraining order against him leading up to the court case gave me a much-needed 6-month respite from his harassing texts and phone calls at all hours of the day and night.

Having that restraining order gave me time and space to heal, move on with my life, and feel less afraid than I had in years. Filing the charges was worth it for that alone.

Of course, I wish that I had won the case and been awarded a permanent restraining order. That would have made my life easier in terms of moving on from that relationship.

Even though things went badly with my court case, I think that standing up for yourself can be the right thing to do. It helped to give me a feeling of closure, and knowing that you did all I could get justice for myself, and to possibly protect another person from being abused by my ex in the future.

Finding Healing

Chapter 17

Finding Healing After Life with a Narcissist

There are many broken pieces of our lives after we have lived with a narcissistic parent, spouse or other family member for any length of time. After all of the crazy making of living with a narcissist, it can take some time to heal.

You may want to consider working with a professional to find healing. There are many strategies that you can use to heal from some of the issues that result from being in a relationship with a narcissist.

Going No-Contact.

If the Gray Rock technique and setting boundaries haven't worked, as a very last resort, you may decide to go no-contact with a narcissist in your life. That is what I have done, and even though I regularly question this, my therapist has repeatedly told me that it was the right thing to do. If you have suffered through years of narcissistic abuse, many therapists will recommend cutting the narcissist out of your life as a first step towards healing.

A narcissist is unlikely to change their harmful behavior.

It is up to you to decide how you will handle this situation. It requires a lot of introspection, looking at their behavior, and asking yourself if you can cope with their repeated demands, manipulation, and otherwise bad behavior.

Sometimes, for various reasons, you may not want to cut off contact. It is very emotionally difficult to go no-contact. It took me years to cut off contact with my narcissistic mother, even after I had realized that she was a narcissist and not likely to change.

I made many attempts to repair my relationship with my mother as an adult. However, none of them were successful, and I couldn't get her to treat me any better even when it was clear that I had changed many of my own behaviors which she found problematic in the past. The problem wasn't me. The problem was her, and her perception of me. Neither of which was ever going to change. I gave her 30+ years to change, and she never did.

Instead of no contact, you may want to have limited contact, or very limited contact, if you feel that there is some good to the relationship to outweigh the bad. This is a very personal decision, and ultimately it is up to you but you may want to talk over both with your partner or friends, and with a therapist. That way, you have other viewpoints besides your own to judge the degree of harm that is being done by the narcissist's behavior.

You may also write up a pros and cons list so that you can see if the costs of staying in contact outweigh the benefits. If one list is much longer than the other, it can give you a clear indication as to which course of action you will want to take.

Whatever you decide to do, it is important to have support, as limiting or cutting contact with a family member is very difficult and painful. In addition to support from your partner and a therapist, there are also many online support groups where you can go to talk to others who are or have been in similar situations. Making sure you aren't alone is extremely important and empowering.

Chapter 18

Grieving the Relationship

I feel like I am still moving through the stages of grief for the mother that I never had. The normal, loving mother that I wished for. The hope that someday my mother would love me.

I grieve for the small child that could never find her place in the world. A child whose innocence was either lost too early, or never existed at all. I grieve for the child who never felt safe.

On TV you see shows like the Gilmore Girls where the mother and daughter are best friends. I wanted a mother like that. A mother who loved me fiercely. A mother who would always go to bat for me, be in my corner no matter what.

My real mother was never in my corner.

I went through stages of grief when I realized that she would never be able to love me the way that I needed. Hurt, anger, resentment, so many feelings. I wanted to heal. To leave the past behind.

According to the University of Washington,

Persistent, traumatic grief can cause us to cycle (sometimes quickly) through the stages of grief: denial, anger, bargaining, depression, acceptance. These stages are our attempts to process change and protect ourselves while we adapt to a new reality. While there are consistent elements within each stage, the process of grieving looks different for everyone.

Now, my mother is an ocean away and I am still thinking about her. Still grieving. Still wishing that I could have had a normal childhood.

The mother that I had never loved me, we never had an emotional bond.

I have tried accepting that she is just a narcissist and I am the scapegoat. Someday, I hope to have a more full sense of acceptance. But today, my heart is like a scar scratched open.

When you are grieving, you can go for a time without thinking about it. The thoughts get fewer and less frequent. The scars heal with time. But still they remain. The thoughts come unbidden at the strangest times.

Sure, I was the one who stopped talking. But she didn't listen even when I was speaking. So, you tell me, who abandoned who.

Healing from grief takes time, and it is important to be kind and gentle with yourself as you are healing. Grieving a relationship or grieving someone who hasn't died is just as real and impactful of a loss as if the person had died, because they are no longer in your life anymore.

According to <u>University of Washington,</u>

Generally, if we are not in the stage of acceptance then we are in some way fighting against or avoiding reality. We might start sleeping more. Our mood or anxious thoughts might become the focus of attention, distracting from external stressors. We might use alcohol or drugs to avoid or disconnect from reality. We might keep our focus on tasks, responsibilities, or the needs of others – staying busy as much as possible to avoid feeling distress.

It is important to give yourself space to heal and realize that you will still grieve for the lost relationship even when you are the one who has decided to cut off contact. It is never an easy decision to make, no matter how warranted it is because of the narcissist's behavior towards you.

The stages of grief are not always linear, and you may move from one stage to another several times before you are finally at peace with the decision to cut off contact with the narcissist in your life.

Chapter 19

Healing From Insecure Attachment

When you have an attachment style other than secure attachment, it can be helpful to go to individual, couples or family therapy. This allows you to have a safe space to discuss your personal attachment issues, and the resulting relationship issues that may ensue.

My attachment issues came up in therapy since I am coping with <u>PTSD</u> from <u>childhood trauma</u>. When I asked my therapist what I could do about my attachment style, he recommended that both my partner and I read <u>Wired for Love</u>.

In the book, it discusses how your adult relationships can help you change your attachment style for the better. This was helpful for me because my partner has a secure attachment style. He is the calm to my storm. His consistency has helped me learn how to trust, open up, and to talk things through in a conflict instead of running away.

If you and your partner both have insecure attachment styles, you can still work together to learn to have a secure attachment style through open communication and trust. Forming a basis of trust is key as the basis of a secure attachment.

Learning to communicate about feelings without blame or judgment is an important first step in creating a healthy relationship. Trust is important because it allows us to feel safe in opening up. When we talk about feelings, we make ourselves vulnerable, and in our relationship with our partners we should be able to do that.

For those of us that didn't grow up with healthy relationship templates, we seldom have the level of trust needed for good communication. So, we have to learn to trust gradually as we come to feel safer with our partners.

If we are single, communication skills can also be practiced with a therapist, close friends, co-workers or in a support group. You can practice good communication skills with anyone in your life, without the need for them to be a romantic partner. In fact, it can be good to take time out from being in relationships for a while after a relationship with a narcissist, and to strengthen our friendships and other support systems.

All in all, good communication can help us in every relationship, not just romantic relationships. As we learn to have better communication skills, we can relate better to family, friends, coworkers, and our children as well.

Chapter 20

How to Heal from Emotional Neglect

If you have symptoms of childhood emotional neglect described earlier, there are ways that you can heal. It is quite common for children of narcissists to experience Childhood Emotional Neglect in addition to other symptoms.

There are several strategies that Dr. Jonice Webb outlines in her book, Running on Empty, including,

1. *Learning to understand and name feelings*
2. *Taking time for Self-Care*
3. *Giving Your child what you never got*

All these skills are extremely helpful in learning how to heal from Childhood Emotional Neglect and overcome a lifetime of living with Narcissistic Parents.

FEELING YOUR FEELINGS

It is incredible the amount of people who feel cut off from their own feelings, or what is referred to as **Alexithymia**. This means, you stop yourself from feeling your feelings.

As discussed in previous chapters, in childhood, many of us are taught in various ways that feelings are bad, and to be avoided at all costs. As a result, there are many of us who, in adulthood, aren't even able to name what we are feeling. This is quite common for adult children of narcissists. If everything in our lives revolves around the narcissist, often our feelings can be seen as inconvenient and a nuisance to them.

Often, we especially learn to avoid negative feelings like anger or sadness, and will instead pretend to be happy, no matter our circumstances. This can put us out of touch with our real feelings, until they explode in moments of stress.

Being unable to name a range of feelings is something that I dealt with myself in therapy, after having told my therapist, "I think that I feel..."

He said to me, "You are so out of touch with your own feelings that you don't even know what you feel. You are trying to name what you think that you should feel. You need to feel your feelings."

Years later, now I know that feelings just *are*. There isn't anything specific that you should be feeling in each moment. Allowing yourself to feel all your feelings, and accepting them, is a huge first step towards healing.

As human beings, we are built to experience a range of emotions. Accepting that all your feelings are normal can be quite a journey. First, we can learn to name our feelings, and then we can learn to accept them.

One exercise that my therapist used with me in allowing myself to name and feel my feelings was a chart of feeling faces. I would look at the chart to see how I was feeling, and what felt closest to my experience at any given time.

Using a list of different feelings and reading through what they mean can also be helpful. When I first started trying to name my feelings, all I could think of was happy, sad and mad. There are so many other emotions though and learning about the whole range of your feelings can broaden and enrich your experience of yourself and your life.

According to Psychology Today,

It is clear from affective neuroscience research that emotions are connected to our evolutionary motivation system. Feelings signal how we are reading the environment, and they are designed to mobilize and drive an adaptive behavioral response.

When we are disconnected from our feelings, we may not react in appropriate ways in a range of situations. We may also be missing out on good feelings as well when we attempt to squelch our bad feelings.

Psychology Today continues,

New learning also happens when we develop the capacity to be with difficult feelings. Because many of our threat-related beliefs and feelings are based on the past, if we continue to obey them and avoid, we won't have the opportunity for new experiential learning to update our beliefs and discover what we are capable of now. In other words, what we avoid we can't learn from. To move beyond our past, we have to engage in new experiences that often feel risky and generate negative feelings like anxiety (in CBT, this is called an "exposure"). This is how we transform old, unhelpful beliefs at an emotional level, and grow in new ways.

As we learn to process and accept our feelings, we can live a much richer experience of life. We can also learn how to develop our emotional intelligence and get along better with all of the people in our lives.

PRACTICE SELF-CARE

When it comes to **Self-Care**, there is so much written about how to care for all the aspects of yourself, especially on social media where it has become a buzzword. But it is important to keep in mind that self-care is more than taking bubble baths with a glass of wine (although if that is what you like, it can be a form of self-care!).

A big "ah-ha" moment for me came when I realized that, as another later therapist told me, "Setting boundaries is self-care."

Before that, I had been getting irritated with both of my therapists for how often they asked me about self-care. I didn't understand everything that self-care encompassed. It felt selfish and frivolous when I had things that needed to be done.

Having a good idea about what works for you in terms of self-care is another way that you can learn to heal.

There are many different forms of self-care that may be helpful for you, and it is important to build self-care as a non-negotiable every day.

For a long time, you have been making a lot of sacrifices, and putting yourself last. When you begin to put yourself first again, it will go a long way towards making you feel validated and rebuilding your mental health.

There are many different ways that you can take care of yourself, but there are five major categories of self-care.

According to <u>Very Well Mind</u> these include,

1. *Physical Self-Care*
2. *Social Self-Care*
3. *Mental Self-Care*
4. *Spiritual Self-Care*
5. *Emotional Self-Care*

All of these different aspects of self-care can help you to feel more well and happier in your daily life. Taking some time each day for self-care and incorporating different types of self-care in your routine can be extremely beneficial for your overall health and happiness.

Personally, I like to practice self-care first thing in the morning. This is my way of making myself a priority. It also helps to set a positive tone for the day.

Some ways to practice self-care can include: saying affirmations, journaling, exercise, yoga, meditation, calling a friend, taking a walk, spending time in nature, or anything else that makes you feel good!

Taking time for your friends, hobbies and interests is also important. Immersing yourself in relationships with people that care about you and doing things that you love will help you feel more balanced. It can also help you feel energized about life again!

Chapter 21

Healing from an Abusive Relationship

Healing from an Abusive Relationship

Breaking the cycle and getting well can begin when you leave the abuse behind and begin to heal yourself. It is important to get support and therapy.

If you have just left, or are leaving, an abusive relationship you can get help from a local women's shelter. If you look up the information on your home computer and you are still in danger, be sure to use an incognito browser, so that your abuser can't track your browsing history.

Women's shelters will help you with not only a place to stay, but with finding therapy as well. Having a counselor or psychiatrist can help you learn new coping skills and look at yourself in a new way.

Once you realize that the abuse was never your fault, you can begin a new and better life.

According to <u>Psych Central</u>, some ways to heal after an abusive relationship include,

· *Creating a safety plan*

- *Set boundaries*
- *Prioritize self-care and self-love*
- *Repeat healing affirmations*
- *Educate yourself about abuse*
- *Build a strong support system*
- *Ask for help*

Going to group therapy or joining an online support group may be helpful as well, so that you can connect with other survivors and discuss coping strategies. It helps to connect with others who have been in similar circumstances, since they can better understand what you have gone through than the average population

One of the biggest things that you may be looking for after leaving an abusive relationship is validation for your feelings and your experience.

Chapter 22

How to Validate
Yourself Again

How do You Validate Yourself After Suffering Narcissistic Abuse?

Learning to care for yourself and your mental health is key after a relationship with a narcissist

Photo by Luis Galvez on Unsplash

After you have dealt with narcissistic abuse, you probably feel very emotionally and psychologically depleted. That was the case for me.

Since there have been several narcissists in my life, there was one thing in common between all of them. Their behavior was invalidating.

Narcissistic Manipulation and Gaslighting

When you have to cope with narcissistic manipulation and gaslighting on a regular basis, it can begin to chip away at your self-esteem. You start to feel fragile, and constantly second-guess yourself.

Over time, this can have a really damaging effect on your psychological and emotional health. It can lead to conditions like anxiety, depression and PTSD.

Getting Help

When you are being gaslighted by a narcissist, it is important to seek help from a therapist. You may also consider reducing contact with the narcissist.

As I have said before, I don't talk to my narcissistic mother anymore, due to advice from multiple mental health professionals. When people have intentionally abused you for years, they are very unlikely to change.

Becoming aware of the abusive patterns is the first step, then you need to decide what you are going to do.

Some people will tell you that you need to forgive the narcissist and maintain the relationship. However, in the long term this may be harmful. You may *want* to forgive your parents and try to move past this, though this is difficult, but it is alright if you don't want to!

According to <u>Psychology Today</u>,

I am by no means suggesting that grown children ought to forgive their parents. While true <u>forgiveness</u> is therapeutic, and we do sometimes, upon reflecting on abusive parents' circumstances, discover reasons to take pity on them and to forgive, adult sons and daughters may or may not have it in them to forgive. Neither is forgiveness ever owed by victims to abusers, whatever the abusers' circumstances.

If you want to maintain a relationship with the narcissist, you will probably need to have some very difficult conversations with them and set firm <u>boundaries</u>.

Finding Validation for Yourself

In order to find validation for yourself again after a relationship with a narcissist, you will need to find your inner strength again.

One of the first sources of strength can be the realization that you were strong enough to walk away from a very toxic person, even though it was probably very difficult to do so.

Knowing that you were strong enough to walk away can become a source of pride, and the beginning of renewing your inner strength.

According to <u>Psychology Today</u>,

Self-validation is accepting your own internal experience, your thoughts, and your feelings. Self-validation doesn't mean that you believe your thoughts or think your feelings are justified. There are many times that you will have thoughts that surprise you or that don't reflect your values or what you know is true. You will also have feelings that you know aren't justified. If you fight the thoughts and feelings or judge yourself for having them, then you increase your emotional upset. You'll also miss out on important information about who you are as a person.

Acceptance of yourself, your feelings and your experience can go a long way towards making you feel validated again after a relationship with a narcissist. The more you begin to accept yourself, the more your feelings will begin to change and become more positive again.

Some tips for self-validation, Psychology Today continues, are:

Be present
Accurate reflection
Guessing
Validating by history
Normalizing
Radical Genuineness

In terms of learning to be present, practicing mindfulness can be very helpful. The non-judgement aspect of Mindfulness can be very helpful in validating your feelings as well. Mindfulness is a technique that is much like meditation but can be practiced every day in your life.

PRACTICE SELF-CARE

After a relationship with a narcissist, practicing more self-care than usual is a must! This will help you get back on your feet emotionally, so that you can start feeling like your old self again.

Chapter 23

Moving On

Once you have gotten out of the relationship with the narcissist, congratulate yourself on making this huge first step! Leaving this type of relationship can be extremely difficult because of the narcissist's persistent love-bombing or threats every time that you tried to leave.

It can be helpful to work with a therapist during this time, especially if you still find yourself very upset even as time passes.

Here are some other tips for healing, according to <u>Healthline</u>:

Acknowledge and accept the abuse

Set your boundaries and set them clearly

Prepare for complex emotions

Reclaim your identity

Practice self-compassion

Understand that your feelings may linger

Take care of yourself

Talk to others

Get professional support

It may take time to heal because, when you are in a relationship with a narcissist, they can be extremely manipulative and will likely have gaslighted you frequently. This can leave you questioning yourself in ways that you never would have otherwise.

Taking time for self-care and practicing self-compassion are helpful tools to get you psychologically "back on your feet" and feeling more prepared for the next chapter of your life.

It can also be helpful during this time to start participating in any hobbies that you may have discarded because of the narcissist. Doing things that you love and enjoy can bring positive emotions back into your life to replace all the negative ones that you are experiencing.

When you are in a relationship with a narcissist, it can feel very isolating. That is why strengthening bonds with other people in your life can bring so much healing right now. Building back up other relationships that are positive in your life can help you move past the relationship with the narcissist.

Don't be upset with yourself if your progress seems to move slowly at first, you are processing a lot of emotions right now! At least, that was my experience. It is ok to feel your feelings and take time to grieve for everything that you have lost; both in terms of the relationship, and pieces of yourself that may feel lost too.

Chapter 24

Healing Your Inner Child

How Do You Reparent Yourself as an Adult

Healing Inner Child wounds

Photo by Wix.

When you have gone through childhood trauma, there can be additional issues when you have a child. Experiences with your children can sometimes be triggering. This can happen when certain experiences remind you of your own childhood in some way.

For example, if you have trouble coping with your feelings, it may prove difficult for you when your child expresses big emotions. This may mean that you will be learning emotional regulation skills along with your child. In this example, using deep breathing techniques with your child, or discussing good ways to handle feelings can be helpful.

If you feel like it is difficult for you to engage with your child this way, there are a host of children's books that can be used to aid in the conversations that you will have with your little one.

When you grew up with narcissistic, abusive or neglectful parenting, it may mean that you never had good adult role models to show you all the basic adulting skills, how to manage your emotions, or how to raise a child. In this case, you will want to become your own adult role model and do things differently than your parents did. This was the case for me when I had kids, so I completely understand.

When you are coping with your own childhood trauma and trying to raise kids, you may want to consider going to therapy for yourself or enrolling in a parenting class to help your kids grow up happy and healthy.

Some strategies that are often used in <u>therapy</u> are called Reparenting and Inner child work. Although they are very similar, there are some slight differences as well.

According to <u>Talkspace</u>, "Reparenting is based on the belief that many <u>psychological issues stem from a child growing up without his or her needs being met</u>. The child is not <u>made to feel secure and unconditionally loved</u>, so they grow up to be an adult who can't navigate relationships and life as well as they should."

Reparenting is often done with a therapist, where they will assume the role of the parent during therapy and attempt to provide a compassionate parental figure. It is much like role-playing in a healthy parent-child relationship.

In contrast, engaging in **Inner Child Work** has to do with showing love to your younger self, as though that young part of yourself were your own child. Using visualization techniques, you can tell the younger you that you love them and are there for them. You can take care of your younger self and keep them safe.

According to Psyche and Soma, *"One of the main components of Inner Child Work is the idea that we all have younger parts within us with different ages, difference experiences, and different needs. As we grow up into bigger bodies and more logical, conscious brains, our younger selves don't just disappear over time. When we get triggered and can't understand why, it's likely a younger part of us is online and very present, screaming for our attention. Oftentimes, as adults, we ignore these cries, we deny or dismiss, we freeze, we search for a solution to "fix it". All of these can be trauma responses being re-played in adult life. We respond to our wounds in ways we learned as a kid and what helped keep us safe* then."

This type of work is often engaged in with the help of a therapist or coach. When I was recovering from my childhood trauma, I worked with my therapist to do EMDR and inner child work. This really helped in my healing process.

Chapter 25

Working With a Therapist

Since a relationship with a narcissist can be extremely psychologically damaging, I would highly recommend working with a therapist or coach after getting out of this type of relationship.

This is especially true if you feel as though you have Anxiety, Depression or PTSD as a result of the time spent in a relationship with a narcissist. These are all serious psychological disorders, and you will get better much more quickly with the assistance of a professional.

I have spent a large portion of my adult life in therapy. Having a therapist is an important way to be able to work through your feelings in a safe and supportive environment.

A therapist is like a guide, that helps you discover the inner workings of yourself.

The therapist can teach you what questions to ask yourself, how to open up when you are afraid and confront those fears, as well as coping skills for a plethora of other issues that you may be experiencing.

Finding a Therapist

When you have a mental health disorder, it can feel very isolating at times. Finding a good therapist can be key to learning coping skills and moving forward towards healing.

As I stated in earlier chapters, I have been diagnosed with PTSD, Anxiety and Depression, partially as a result of narcissistic parents and a relationship with a narcissist in adulthood.

Having a supportive therapist has been very helpful in my healing journey. Talking things through with someone objective has helped me to learn coping skills to become calmer and more peaceful.

I believe that finding a good therapist can be helpful to anyone coping with a mental health condition, including chronic stress. A therapist can also help you understand what has gone wrong in your relationship with a narcissist, and to realize that many of the things that happened were not your fault. Talk therapy is a valuable tool to process through difficult past situations, and learn valuable lessons about what to do differently in the future to have healthier relationship patterns.

MY STRUGGLE TO FIND A THERAPIST.

Before I found my current therapist, I went through a difficult journey to find some help. I had been having panic attacks at work, and I went to the Employee Assistance Program. However, the therapist there couldn't sign off on the FMLA (Family Medical Leave Act) that she had advised me to request. I was told that I needed a signature from a Psychiatrist.

Unfortunately, finding a Psychiatrist is much more difficult than finding a therapist. I went to intakes at several different crisis centers, but I was not admitted to any of them because I wasn't a danger to myself or others. I was provided with a list of Psychiatrists in my local area that take my insurance, so that I could call to get an appointment.

When I got home, my partner and I both called every provider on the list to try to obtain an appointment. The soonest appointment that we could find was three months away.

So, I kept trying to find a mental health provider. I never found a sooner Psychiatrist appointment; however I was able to get an appointment with a therapist and begin treatment for my PTSD.

The sheer number of calls I had to make was sometimes overwhelming, and I was very lucky to have a supportive partner who made many of those calls for me. It was so helpful to have him take over. If you have someone in your life you can rely on, that can make a big difference in your recovery too.

GOING TO A CRISIS CENTER OR EMERGENCY ROOM.

If you are experiencing a mental health crisis, it is important to get help right away! You can do this by calling a crisis line, such as the National Suicide Hotline (800-273-8255) or a local crisis line. When you call the crisis line, they will be able to direct you to the nearest local crisis center.

Or you can walk into any Emergency Room, and let them know that you are experiencing a mental health crisis. When you go into the Emergency Room, they will be able to provide you with immediate care. They may admit you into the hospital or refer you to intensive outpatient treatment.

GET A REFERRAL FROM YOUR DOCTOR.

In the American medical system, finding a therapist can sometimes prove to be very difficult, and often we will have to advocate strongly for our own mental health needs.

If you have a relationship with a primary care doctor, this can be a good place to start. It is often easier to get a prompt appointment with a primary care doctor, and if you already have a longstanding relationship with your doctor, they will be familiar with your medical history as well. When you go to the doctor, you can tell them your mental health symptoms, and they may be able to provide a prescription right away and refer you to a therapist.

Once you have a referral from your primary care doctor, it will be much quicker to get an appointment with a mental health provider. A referral from your doctor may also mean that you will get a therapist who works closely with your doctor, which can be helpful as well.

GET A REFERRAL FROM YOUR INSURANCE COMPANY.

If you don't have a primary care doctor, or if they are unable to give you a referral to a therapist, then it is a good idea to check with your insurance company. This will ensure that when you find a therapist, your visits will be covered by your insurance plan.

Often, your insurance provider will have a website that lists providers who are covered under your plan. On their website, you may be able to search by your area, as well as the specialty of the provider. For example, if you have Anxiety, you can find a provider specializing in anxiety.

Some insurance providers will actually let you book appointments straight from their website. If this isn't the case, you may need to call several different providers to find one that is accepting new patients.

GET A REFERRAL FROM A COMMUNITY AGENCY.

If you don't have insurance, you may be able to get a referral from a community agency. Currently, I attend therapy at what is called a Community Mental Health Center. There are centers like this located in many different states.

When I found my current therapist, I got a referral from the <u>TANF</u> program at my local city office. At the city Human Services office, I was able to apply for other programs like <u>Medicaid</u>, Food Assistance and Job Assistance. Services like this are very helpful if you have become unemployed due to your mental health, or other reasons.

Medicaid is a program that provides free medical insurance to low-income Americans. You can qualify for Medicaid if you are unemployed, or if you are in a certain income range.

Community Mental Health Centers will often accept Medicaid or operate on a sliding fee scale. This is very helpful if you are unemployed, or otherwise low income. Often, a Community Mental Health Center will be much more accessible to many people than a therapist that is in private practice.

ONLINE THERAPY.

If going to a therapist in a traditional office is difficult for you, there are many fully online therapists available today as well.

During the pandemic, I was able to do therapy through Zoom calls to continue my treatment without interruption. Online therapy can be available through your insurance, or through fully online providers.

According to <u>Healthline</u>, here are the top 10 online therapy providers:

- **Best overall:** Talkspace
- **Largest network of licensed counselors:** BetterHelp
- **Best online therapy for cognitive behavioral therapy (CBT):** Online-Therapy.com
- **Best online therapy for mental and physical health:** Amwell

- **Best for online psychiatry:** MDLive
- **Best online therapy for your budget:** 7 Cups
- **Best online therapy for couples:** ReGain
- **Best online therapy for teens:** Teen Counseling
- **Best online therapy for LGBTQ:** Pride Counseling
- **Best online therapy for single video sessions:** Doctor on Demand

Often, it is easier to get an appointment with an online therapist, and these appointments may be cheaper than traditional therapy as well.

CONCLUSION.

Finding a therapist or other mental health professional in the United States can be a daunting task. However, once you understand the steps that you have to follow to navigate the medical system, it can become more manageable.

If you are low income, you can get assistance and referrals from Medicaid. Otherwise, you can get assistance from your primary care doctor, or insurance company.

Note: This is the process for getting mental healthcare in the US. If you are in the UK, you would need to present to an MH specialist. Otherwise, if you just go to any therapist, they may not be able to diagnose a personality disorder.

Eye Movement Desensitization and Reprocessing (EMDR)

One type of therapy that may be helpful if you have experienced trauma or have PTSD because of the relationship with a narcissist is called EMDR. This is a type of therapy that is done in addition to talk therapy, which will assist you in processing through traumatic memories so that they will no longer be as emotionally triggering.

According to EMDR,

EMDR (Eye Movement Desensitization and Reprocessing) is a psychotherapy that enables people to heal from the symptoms and emotional distress that are the result of disturbing life experiences. Repeated studies show that by using EMDR therapy people can experience the benefits of psychotherapy that once took years to make a difference. It is widely assumed that severe emotional pain requires a long time to heal. EMDR therapy shows that the mind can in fact heal from psychological trauma much as the body recovers from physical trauma. When you cut your hand, your body works to close the wound. If a foreign object or repeated injury irritates the wound, it festers and causes pain. Once the block is removed, healing resumes. EMDR therapy demonstrates that a similar sequence of events occurs with mental processes. The brain's information processing system naturally moves toward mental health. If the system is blocked or imbalanced by the impact of a disturbing event, the emotional wound festers and can cause intense suffering. Once the block is removed, healing resumes. Using the detailed protocols and procedures learned in EMDR therapy training sessions, clinicians help clients activate their natural healing processes.

When you have an EMDR session, you will pick a particular traumatic memory to work on for that session. Your therapist will ask you on a scale of 1-10 how upsetting the memory is for you. They will ask you what negative thought is associated with the memory, and how you would like to think instead. Then, they will ask you where you feel the sensation in your body that is associated with the memory.

Therapists will use assistive devices like buzzers that you hold in your hand during the session. This is to assist you in feeling in touch with your body during the session. Then, the therapist will guide you through the traumatic memory, having you remember as if you were actually there. This allows you to reprocess the traumatic memory.

According to <u>Very Well Mind</u>,

While you focused on the targeted memory, your therapist will lead you through stimulation sets. These sets may include eye movements, tactile taps, or auditory tones.

After each stimulation set, your therapist will instruct you to clear your mind and discuss any insights, thoughts, memories, feelings, or images that came to mind. If you're still experiencing negative sensations, they will become the focus of the next set. This process continues until the target memory no longer distresses you.

Having the therapist assist you in going back through each traumatic memory will help you to feel more in control of your reaction to the situation. It can also help you look at the situation in a new light. If you believe that a situation was your fault and you blame yourself for example, it will help to remove the self-blame and replace that with more helpful thoughts and feelings, such as self-acceptance and compassion.

Processing traumatic memories this way will take away the emotional charge that you feel associated with the memory. This is what is called reprocessing. When you have reprocessed the traumatic memory, you will no longer feel like you are reexperiencing the traumatic event when you recall the memory.

After going to EMDR sessions for several months, I was able to process through my traumatic memories, so that I was no longer feeling triggered when I would think of them. It was a great help to me in speeding up my healing process.

According to Very Well Mind, some of the benefits of EMDR therapy include:

- **Changes negative thinking:** *EMDR can help you identify, challenge, and even change the negative thoughts cluttering your mind.*

- **Decreases chronic pain**: *Research shows that bilateral stimulation activates the region of the brain associated with relaxation and comfortable feelings.*[4]
- **Improves self-esteem**: *EMDR works by targeting distressing memories and negative thoughts associated with yourself. By identifying them, you learn how to process and heal from them.*
- **Requires minimal talking**: *In EMDR, you don't have to divulge every detail of your painful experience like you would in talk therapy. This makes EMDR is particularly useful for people who have difficulty talking about their trauma.*
- **Yields fast results**: *EMDR is classified as a brief-psychotherapy. While everyone's journey is different, 80% to 90% of people report positive results within their first three sessions.*

I have found EMDR very effective for my PTSD, and I would highly recommend seeking out a professional that is proficient in using EMDR therapy if you are experiencing PTSD symptoms yourself.

Chapter 26

Healing Ourselves Makes us Better Parents

Healing Ourselves Makes us Better Parents

When we heal ourselves, it helps us to become better parents too, since we are able to be calmer and more caring.

Even by recognizing that we have unhealed inner child wounds, we are taking the first step towards healing. This is because we have brought our unconscious patterns to a conscious level, which allows us to work on changing them. This means that we can consciously choose to act differently than our parents.

We can choose a different parenting style than our parents had. For example, if your parents were very strict with you, then you can take a more balanced approach to parenting. Or, if your parents ignored you, then you can choose to be more involved with your children.

Also, it can be helpful to learn about different parenting styles through books or classes, so that you can use the most effective parenting strategies with your kids. For example, I have chosen an <u>Attachment Parenting</u> approach with my children, since my parents often left my sister and I alone.

Just the act of consciously choosing to be present with your children, and to make their needs a priority, will make a big difference in their lives.

When we choose to heal our own inner child wounds, we are breaking an unhealthy cycle of generational trauma. As we go through the healing process and become more whole, we can be more peaceful and patient with ourselves and our children as well.

Chapter 27

Is Forgiveness Necessary for Healing?

There are so many self-help guru's online that tell you to forgive the people who have hurt you, so that you can move on. There are motivational quotes all over the place saying the same thing.

I disagree.

I don't think that forgiving people who have hurt you is necessary for healing. It is only necessary if you want to continue having a relationship with those people. Personally, I feel like I have healed a lot more by going no-contact with narcissistic family members than I could have if I forgave them.

This may be an unpopular view, but I think the decision whether to forgive someone who hurts you is a very personal one. You shouldn't feel pressured to forgive someone just because it seems like the 'right thing to do.'

Forgiveness should come from you, and only if that is what you truly want. Don't forgive someone because your family member or therapist tells you to. It should be something that you decide on your own. If you forgive because someone else tells you to, then you are giving up your agency by putting a huge decision into someone else's hands.

As an adult, I have decided that I will no longer forgive people who aren't sorry for their actions.

If people aren't sorry for their actions, if they don't understand that those actions were wrong and hurtful, that means they are going to keep acting in the same way in the future. Many narcissists think that their actions are justified. They think that you deserve to be hurt. That means, they are going to keep on hurting you. No matter how many times you forgive them.

Forgiveness is meaningless without change.

Forgive Yourself Instead

I think that forgiving yourself is much more important for healing than forgiving people that have hurt you.

When you forgive yourself, you are acknowledging that it wasn't your fault that someone harmed you, or you are forgiving yourself for aspects of a problematic situation that you feel responsible for.

According to Better Help,

Forgiveness, whether of someone else or yourself, means you accept actions and behaviors that occurred while willing to move forward. You are eager to move on, knowing you can't change what happened. Forgiving yourself means letting go of the feelings and emotions associated with what went wrong. You let go of any resentment or anger. It may be easier to do this when forgiving others, but many find it hard to do this for themselves.

Forgiving yourself can be difficult when you have been raised to believe that every single problem is your fault. I have struggled with this a lot, but I am improving. For a while, any time I would hear of a problem like people starving in Africa or the war in Ukraine, I would feel like even that must be somehow my fault. I have narrowed it down now to things in my immediate sphere.

When you forgive yourself for the past, then you realize that a lot of things that the narcissist did to you weren't about you. The things that happened, the things they did, were about them.

A Conscious Choice Not to Forgive

I tried to have a better relationship with my mom. I asked her if we could talk about feelings like a normal mother and daughter into my early 30's.

First, she told me, "Our family doesn't do that."

I pushed a little harder. Then she said, "I really hate your ex-husband."

Thanks mom. I wanted to talk about my feelings but let's talk about yours instead. Everything is always all about you.

Honestly, trying to get a narcissist to realize that you have feelings, or that your feelings have any value or basis in reality can be impossible.

When it comes to my mom, I have chosen not to forgive to protect myself and my children. She doesn't even acknowledge that what she did was wrong, or that she hurt me. She is just going to keep on hurting me. Forgiveness opens the door for her to do that.

If you have a narcissist in your life, sometimes the conscious choice not to forgive can help you stand up for yourself. You are finally saying, "No. I will not accept being treated like this. You are not allowed to hurt me anymore."

Forgiving someone who isn't sorry is just a futile exercise in self harm. It harbors the belief that the person in question can change. The problem with this is that for them to change, they must realize that they did something wrong. Narcissists don't believe that they were wrong. Pure and simple.

Chapter 28

Coping With People Thinking Badly of You

When you leave a relationship with a narcissist, they try to spin it like they are the victim, and like they have no clue why you would do something so drastic.

My mom is a covert narcissist most of the time. What I call a "poor me."

She plays the victim so well that other people have always fallen for it. She pretends to be helpless, even though she is just lazy. She is a smart person. She moves up in every job that she gets. She can do just fine for herself.

People have told me that my mother is the nicest person they have ever met.

That was the hardest thing for me to move past. It took years of therapy to do that. She wasn't nice to me. She wasn't nice behind closed doors.

She excused my dad's abuse of me. She told me that it was my fault.

The words still ring in my ears, "If you didn't make him mad, he wouldn't hit you."

How do you let that go? How do you forgive? Somehow, I did it for years.

Occasionally, after I went no-contact, I would see parents of some of my childhood friends, and they always ask how my mom is doing. I would get these crazy looks when I told them that we didn't talk anymore.

I stopped saying that I would just say, "fine." I know she is fine because my daughter talks to her and would tell me if she wasn't. It is easier than dealing with other people's stares and questions about why I don't talk to my mom anymore.

When you leave a relationship with a narcissist, either in your family or a partner, you are likely to be judged harshly by other people in your life who were either flying monkeys of the narcissist, or who just don't understand the situation.

Cutting off a family member is something that is not commonly done in society, and as such people will often think that there is something wrong with you for taking such a drastic step. It can be hurtful to deal with other people's judgment of you for cutting off a toxic relationship.

Depending on the relationship that you have with the other person, you may or may not want to go into a great amount of detail about why you cut off the relationship with the narcissist. You can make a simple, general statement about how the person was toxic, or you can choose not to engage at all. You must do what will protect your mental health.

You may lose quite a few friends after you go no-contact with the narcissist. Typically, since some narcissists can be so charismatic, other people will take their side in the breakup, or try to convince you to get back together. When it is your family, people will be even more insistent that you forgive because "family is forever" and they will expect you to forgive even if the narcissist isn't sorry.

According to <u>Vivian McGrath</u>, after her break up with a narcissist:

I made a decision to open up and nurture friendships with those whom approached me at this time. I'd stop chasing, stop trying to salvage, stop trying to talk as loud he was and stop trying to prove I was a good person, while he was dragging my name through the mud.

It was far too exhausting and in the end, it certainly wasn't worth it. I knew in time my actions would speak volumes and that those who mattered in my life would stick close and others would fall away.

Instead, I tightened up the inner circle of those I love and trusted. I kept them close and I was very careful about giving energy away to anyone else at this time.

I culled at least 100 "friends" from my Facebook account. The ones I didn't know if I could count on or trust at this vulnerable time.

If I felt the slightest bit judged or knew that they were spending time with my ex I had to walk away. I didn't have the energy to fight for friendships. I needed non-judgmental love and support and not to be guessing where I stood with people.

Early on in our separation, I noticed a few "friends" who were there at the scene, hovering like ravens for information and gossip.

Not one of these people stayed around after things simmered down. They simply wanted to feed off the drama in the same way people get addicted to trash magazines or reality shows, but quickly move onto the 'next thing'.

It was similar for me after I broke up with my narcissistic ex. I lost almost all our mutual friends. He came right out and told me that all of our friends were now 'his' friends and that I needed to stop contacting them. I was pretty beaten down at that point, and so I agreed.

At that point, I had to make new friends who didn't know him. Some of these friends have proven to be the best and truest friends that I have today.

Narcissists try to ruin your relationships with everyone. They will paint you as crazy and say that everything that happened was your fault. They will play the innocent victim, and you will find that a lot of people will believe them.

Difficult though it may be, you may want to consider cutting off contact with any of the flying monkeys as well, otherwise the narcissist may continue using them indefinitely to harass you indirectly using shame and blame tactics.

Even if people have never known the narcissist at all, or have never had contact with them, they may still judge you because of your choice to go no-contact. It seems too extreme for people to wrap their minds around. It is understandable I suppose, since most people will never go through the crazy making that is a relationship with a narcissist. They have no way to understand how you feel afterward, and so they judge you instead of trying to understand.

If you want to focus on your healing, it is important to have people in your life who genuinely love and support you. Otherwise, you will still be on high alert all the time and in fear of saying or doing the wrong thing that will get back to the narcissist.

Cutting off contact with the narcissist may mean cutting off contact with other people who are still in regular contact with them as well. Again, in the case of individual relationships that you may be choosing to cut off, you may want to talk through this with your therapist to make sure you are doing what will best protect your mental health.

Chapter 29

How Do You Find Love After Narcissistic Abuse?

It starts with learning how to love yourself again

A fter a relationship with a narcissist, you may want to put yourself back out there in the dating pool again right away. But, this isn't just another break-up.

A relationship with a narcissist can be emotionally damaging in so many ways, it is better to take some time to work on yourself and get back to feeling good again on your own before you seek out a new relationship.

Sometimes, it can be easy to seek out validation again from a new relationship, but it is better to find internal validation. This is because internal validation is more lasting, and not dependent on another person.

Finding Self-Love Again

When you have been in a relationship with a narcissist, it is likely they have been making you doubt yourself a lot. It can be a crushing blow to your self-esteem.

Finding your way back to yourself is an important first step before taking on a new relationship with someone else.

According to the <u>Brain and Behavior Foundation,</u>

Self-love is a <u>state of appreciation for oneself</u> that grows from actions that support our physical, psychological and spiritual growth. Self-love means having a high regard for your own well-being and happiness. Self-love means taking care of your own needs and not sacrificing your well-being to please others. Self-love means not settling for less than you deserve.

Since in a relationship with a narcissist, you often settle for less than you deserve, building new standards for how you allow others to treat you is an important part of cultivating self-love again after the relationship has ended.

Brain and Behavior continues.

Ways to practice self-love include:

Becoming mindful. People who have more self-love tend to know what they think, feel, and want.

Taking actions based on need rather than want. By staying focused on what you need, you turn away from automatic behavior patterns that get you into trouble, keep you stuck in the past, and lessen self-love.

Practicing good self-care. You will love yourself more when you take better care of your basic needs. People high in self-love nourish themselves daily through healthy activities, like sound nutrition, exercise, proper sleep, intimacy and healthy social interactions.

Making room for healthy habits. Start truly caring for yourself by mirroring that in what you eat, how you exercise, and what you spend time doing. Do stuff, not to "get it done" or because you "have to," but because you care about you.

Taking care of your mind, body and spirit are good ways to learn to practice self-love again.

When you practice self-care, and take good care of your body and mind, you will be more at peace inside yourself. This can help you feel centered, grounded, and validated within yourself.

Learning to Trust Yourself

Before you get into a new relationship, it is important to learn to trust yourself and your decisions again.

If you are anything like me, being in a relationship with a narcissist can make you doubt your own decision-making skills, and your ability to judge the character of others.

It is important to build up your self-confidence and learn to trust yourself again before you decide to get into a relationship with someone new. Otherwise, you are going to be constantly second-guessing the relationship because you don't trust yourself to make good decisions about relationships.

According to Healthline,

Trusting yourself can build up your confidence, make it easier for you to make decisions, and reduce your stress levels.

As you work on learning to trust yourself again with small decisions, you will build up confidence in your own decision-making abilities and trust yourself more with big decisions.

Here are 6 tips that Healthline gives for learning to trust yourself more:

Be yourself

Set reasonable goals

Be kind to yourself

Build on your strengths

Spend time with yourself

Be decisive

Taking time alone to focus on yourself, and on learning to trust yourself again will help you to feel more confident again, and to replenish your self-esteem.

Working on yourself and learning self-love and self-acceptance before you get into another relationship is key to ensuring that you are mentally and emotionally healthy before you get into a new relationship. Otherwise, you may still be carrying some of your feelings from your relationship with the narcissist into your next relationship, and it can lead to problems which will keep the new relationship from progressing.

You need to be able to trust yourself before you will be able to trust another person completely, as a relationship requires.

Ask What You Want from a New Relationship

Once you are feeling better with yourself, and you are calm and centered again, you can begin to ask yourself what it is that you want from a new relationship. That way, you will know what you are looking for in a partner before you get back into the dating pool.

After I got out of a relationship with a narcissist, the most important thing for me was finding someone who was nice to me every day.

Consistency.

When you are with a narcissist, life is like a roller coaster ride, and you never know where it is going to take you. So, in my next relationship, I looked for someone that I knew I would be able to depend on all the time.

You can make a list of the qualities that you are looking for, by thinking about what is important for you in a relationship.

Do you want someone with a sense of humor? Someone who will share your hobbies with you? Someone who would be a good parent? Likes to travel?

The possibilities are endless.

Once you think of the personality traits that are important to you in a potential partner, you will be able to tell more easily if someone is going to be a good fit for you earlier in the relationship.

Don't Ignore Red Flags

There are a lot of red flags when you get into a relationship with a narcissist, but often we overlook them.

When you are meeting new people, it is important to look not just at how they treat you, but how they treat others around them. Are they polite to waitresses and other service people? Do they have a good relationship with their parents? Long term friends?

All of these are indicators that someone has a good personality across a variety of situations.

Also, it is important to note how they talk about other people. If they are constantly complaining about their ex or their boss, this is an indication that they tend to blame others for their problems, instead of taking responsibility for themselves.

These, and many other things can be red flags at the start of a new relationship.

In my case, when I first started dating again, I decided that I wanted a guy who had his own house, car and a job. So, it was a red flag for me when I went on two dates with a guy, and he proceeded to ask me to borrow money.

Depending on your own goals for a relationship, different things will be red flags for you. But, remember that anything that makes you feel uncomfortable can be a reason to walk away.

It may mean that this isn't the right partner for you, or that you aren't ready to be dating again yet.

Chapter 30

But what about kids who are suffering in toxic fam

Do you know a child that is suffering in a toxic family or being raised by a narcissist?

Often, these children will be removed from their parents. This is especially true in cases where there is drug use or abuse.

Children who have been removed from their families and are then put into the Foster Care System in the United States. Since the pandemic hit, there are more children than ever in need of foster homes.

If you have a child like this in your family, you can offer to be a foster parent for them, if you choose. If this is something you are considering, it is important to consult with legal counsel to find out the proper procedures to follow, as these will differ based on where you live.

If you do adopt a child in need, it is important to remember that, like yourself, these children have experienced trauma, and will need additional support.

It is important to put children who have suffered trauma into therapy as soon as possible, so that they will be able to heal.

Children are very resilient, and the sooner that they can get some help, the faster and easier their healing will be.

Chapter 31

References

How Being Raised By A Narcissist Damages Your Life And Self-Esteem (forbes.com)

Prevalence, Correlates, Disability, and Comorbidity of DSM-IV Narcissistic Personality Disorder: Results from the Wave 2 National Epidemiologic Survey on Alcohol and Related Conditions - PMC (nih.gov)

Why Is Everyone's Ex Suddenly a Narcissist? | Psychology Today

Narcissistic personality disorder - Symptoms and causes - Mayo Clinic

10 Signs of a Narcissistic Parent | Psychology Today

Effects of Narcissistic Abuse (verywellmind.com)

Amazon.com: Running on Empty: Overcome Your Childhood Emotional Neglect: 9781614482420: Webb, Jonice, Musello, Christine: Books

Long-Term Narcissistic Abuse Can Cause Brain Damage (psychcentral.com)

What to Do If You or a Loved One Lack Empathy (verywellmind.com)

Manipulation: 7 Signs to Look For (webmd.com)

What are Flying Monkeys? - Narcissist Abuse Support

Gaslighting in Families: Signs of Gaslighting Parents (psycom.net)

Gaslighting: What it is, long-term effects, and what to do (medicalnewstoday.com)

What to Know About Perfectionist Parenting (verywellfamily.com)

No laughing matter: Some perfectionists have a dark side -- ScienceDaily

From hero to zero: How narcissistic perfectionists hurt those around them - Dal News - Dalhousie University

What to Know About Perfectionist Parenting (verywellfamily.com)

Golden child and scapegoat - daughters of narcissistic mothers

Why Do Narcissists Have a Golden Child and Scapegoat Child? (thenarcissisticlife.com)

Covert Narcissist: Signs, Causes, and How to Respond (verywellmind.com)

What Is Covert Narcissistic Abuse? Gaslighting, Manipulation, And Intimidation | BetterHelp

Narcissists And Animals - Narcissisms.Com

Attachment Styles and Their Role in Adult Relationships (attachmentproject.com)

Grey Rocking: What this Method is and How To Do It (and when not to) (betterup.com)

How to Set Boundaries With a "Narcissist" — Talkspace

How To Go Low Contact With Your Narcissistic Mother? - The Narcissistic Life

Can Narcissists Love? | Psych Central

What Narcissists Really Think About Their Partners | Psychology Today

In a Relationship with a Narcissist? A Guide to Narcissistic Relationships (psychalive.org)

What is a Narcissistic Abuse Cycle & How Does It Work? - Choosing Therapy

Most dangerous time for battered women? When they leave. (clarionledger.com)

Create a Safety Plan | The National Domestic Violence Hotline (thehotline.org)

Will My Partner Be Violent After I Leave? (domesticshelters.org)

Colorado Civil Assist – Civil Standbys in Domestic Violence Cases - Denver Criminal Attorney Specializing in Domestic Violence Cases - Colorado Criminal Defense Lawyer. (colorado-domestic-violence-lawyer.com)

Relationship Violence | Types of Crimes (usf.edu)

The Stages of Grief: Accepting the Unacceptable | Counseling Center (washington.edu)

Wired for Love: How Understanding Your Partner's Brain and Attachment Style Can Help You Defuse Conflict and Build a Secure Relationship: Tatkin PsyD MFT, Stan, Hendrix PhD, Harville: 9781608820580: Amazon.com: Books

5 Self-Care Practices for Every Area of Your Life (verywellmind.com)

How to Heal After an Abusive Relationship: 7 Tips | Psych Central

When Parents Offer Gaslighting Instead of Love | Psychology Today

9 Tips, Tools, and Strategies for Narcissistic Abuse Recovery (healthline.com)

What Is Reparenting & Why Should You Consider It? — Talkspace

What is Inner Child Work? - Psyche and Soma Psychotherapy Group (psycheandsomatherapy.com)

Family and Medical Leave Act | U.S. Department of Labor (dol.gov)

Temporary Assistance for Needy Families (TANF) | The Administration for Children and Families (hhs.gov)

How to Apply for Medicaid and CHIP | USAGov

10 Top Online Therapy Picks for 2022 (healthline.com)

EMDR Therapy: Uses, Techniques, and Effectiveness (verywellmind.com)

Narcissistic abuse recovery means losing friends - Vivian Mcgrath

Self-Love and What It Means | Brain & Behavior Research Foundation (bbrfoundation.org)

Trusting Yourself: 6 Tips to Build It (healthline.com)

Chapter 32

About the Author

Nicole Dake is a blogger, author, and mom of three. Nicole blogs about parenting with a focus on health & wellness for moms and kids. Nicole has a BA in Psychology with a minor in Religious Studies from University of Colorado, Paralegal Certification from Boston University. Currently located in Frankfurt, Germany. Originally from the US.

Open to collaboration.

Published works: Trauma Survivor's Guide to Coping With Panic Attacks (2021), Happy. Healthy. Rich. The smart mom's guide to living your best life. (2021) and The Way Things Go, A book of poems (2022), Daily Positive Affirmations (2022).

Awards: BookFest Award for best Mental Health Book 2022 for Trauma Survivor's Guide to Coping With Panic Attacks.

Blog: https://medium.com/@nicoledake

Contact: coloradogirl750@gmail.com

Newsletter: https://nicoledake.substack.com/

Want to join my affiliate program?

https://payhip.com/auth/register/af629252a3362d7

Trauma Survivor's Guide

to Coping with Panic Attacks

Focusing on Panic Associated with PTSD and cPTSD

Nicole Dake

PTSD controlled my life - no more. I once was a survivor, now I'm a warrior.

Panic attacks that result from PTSD and cPTSD can be debilitating. Research unfortunately falls short, telling those suffering from panic attacks to just "wait for them to be over." Over the years I have learned to cope, first preparing for panic attacks, and then calming down during a panic attack. I am sharing these coping skills with others who have PTSD, so they can go from being survivors to warriors too.

Available on Amazon, Barns & Noble, and wherever books are sold.